90 Days to
Possessing
Your Healing

DESTINY IMAGE BOOKS BY KYNAN BRIDGES

Possessing Your Healing

Supernatural Favor

90 Days to

Possessing
Your Healing

KYNAN BRIDGES

DESTINY IMAGE® PUBLISHERS, INC.

P.O. Box 310, Shippensburg, PA 17257-0310

"Promoting Inspired Lives."

This book and all other Destiny Image, Revival Press, MercyPlace, Fresh Bread, Destiny Image Fiction, and Treasure House books are available at Christian bookstores and distributors worldwide.

For a U.S. bookstore nearest you, call 1-800-722-6774.

For more information on foreign distributors, call 717-532-3040.

Reach us on the Internet: www.destinyimage.com.

ISBN 13 TP: 978-0-7684-0412-8

ISBN 13 Ebook: 978-0-7684-0413-5

For Worldwide Distribution, Printed in the U.S.A.

1 2 3 4 5 6 7 8 / 18 17 16 15 14

ACKNOWLEDGMENTS

First of all, I want to acknowledge my Lord and Savior Jesus Christ, through whom I am empowered to write this book. To my wife and ministerial staff, thank you! Special thanks to the editorial and production team at Destiny Image, including Ronda Ranalli, Terri Meckes, and Dominique Abney, to name but a few.

I also want to take a moment and acknowledge the great men and women of the faith who have impacted my life and ministry in a positive way (either directly or indirectly), including Smith Wigglesworth, John G. Lake, Oswald Chambers, John Wesley, Jack Coe, Oral Roberts, Kathryn Kuhlman, R. W. Shambach, Kenneth E. Hagin, Wayne C. Thompson, Dr. T. L. Osborn, Dr. Martin Luther King Jr., Heidi Baker, Bill Johnson, Dr. Mark Chironna, Randy Clark, Mahesh Chavda, Hank Kunneman, Apostle G. Maldanado, Sid Roth, Rabbi Jonathan Bernis, Apostle Charles Ndifon, Dr. Charles and Francis Hunter, Joan Hunter, Pastor Marlin D. Harris, Dr. E. V. Hill, Dr. Barbie Breathitt, Mike Bickle, Pastor Andre Mitchell,

Apostle Mark T. Jones, Marilyn Hickey, John Loren Sanford, Dr. T. L. Lowery, Dr. Douglas Wingate, Benny Hinn, and Evangelist Reinhard Bonnke. Thank you for your service and gift to the body of Christ. God bless you!

FOREWORD

Very few Bible believers understand how to receive a healing or even how biblical faith operates. With what is coming to America in the next few years, it is urgent that you understand and walk in true faith. Pastor Kynan Bridges has taught his entire church how to walk in genuine Bible faith. Now he wants to pour this God-directed teaching into your life. Jesus promised that you will do the same works as He did—and even greater works (see John 14:12). That's "normal" as defined by the Bible. I want you to be normal!

Sid Roth, Host
It's Supernatural! Television

Day 1

HIS AUTHORITY IN YOU

HEALING MEDITATION

*Behold, I give unto you power to tread on
serpents and scorpions, and over all the
power of the enemy: and nothing shall by
any means hurt you.* —Luke 10:19

There are times in life when we face difficulties and challenges, sometimes even in our physical bodies. It is in these moments we need to be reminded the most that we have authority. Jesus told His disciples in the Gospel of Luke that He gave them authority, which is the Greek word *exousia* (Strong's, G1849). The best way to understand this concept is to imagine an officer of the law. They are given a badge to signify and symbolize the legal authority they possess. In essence, the officer carries the full authority of the governing body he or she represents. When a criminal trespasses against this officer, they have the legal right to resist the criminal. In much the same way, you and I have been given authority by God to resist the powers of darkness in the form of sickness and disease in our lives. You are not a victim. You are a victor, because greater is He that lives in you than He that is in the world (see 1 John 4:4). Instead of allowing the sickness, disease, infirmity, or ailment to take control over you, take control over it. Just as the officer has the full resources of the government at his disposal when arresting a criminal, you have the full backing of the kingdom of God when arresting sickness. Take authority today!

HEALING PRAYER

Father, in the name of Your Son Jesus Christ, I thank You for who You are and all that You have done. I thank You for the authority that I possess in You. Right now, I take authority over every symptom, ailment, infirmity, and sickness in my body and in the bodies of those I love. I declare that according to Luke 10:19, You have given me the legal right to resist Satan and all of his power in my life. I declare that in the name of Jesus Christ, nothing shall by any means harm me. Fear, worry, anxiety, and guilt have no power over me. I command all lying symptoms to cease. I command pain to go and any and all growths to dry up in the name of Jesus. Today I serve notice to sickness and disease (spiritual, emotional, or physical), that it is under arrest. I come in the full authority of the kingdom of God and the name of Jesus, and declare that I am free from the oppressive hand of the enemy. I am the healed of the Lord, in Jesus's name. Amen!

IT IS FINISHED!

HEALING MEDITATION

When Jesus therefore had received the vinegar,
He said, It is finished: and He bowed His
head, and gave up the ghost. —John 19:30

As a kid I remember sitting in the classroom and taking final examinations. Usually, there would be a proctor or teacher present. Their task was to monitor the students and make sure that no one cheated on the exam. One of the aspects of taking an exam I vividly remember was submitting the completed test to the proctor. We would raise our hand and say, "I am finished." Once you submitted your exam to the proctor, you couldn't make any additional changes. When Jesus was on the cross two thousand years ago, He took the penalty of our sin upon Himself, and when the wrath of God was fully satisfied, He declared, "It is finished." This Greek word *teleo* means to bring something to a complete close or to fulfill in time (Strong's, G5055). Jesus paid the ultimate price. He satisfied our debt in its entirety. He brought the season of God's wrath to a close. As far as heaven is concerned, our test has been submitted to the proctor and no more changes can be made. This means God will never use sickness or disease to punish us. We are no longer under God's wrath. Never allow the enemy to tell you that you deserve what is coming against you because of your sin. You don't have to earn your healing; it is already finished. Receive your healing today in Jesus's name.

HEALING PRAYER

Father, in the name of Jesus, I thank You for Your mercy and loving-kindness. Lord, I now accept the finished work of Jesus Christ as the final payment of my sin, and I no longer allow Satan to torment me with sickness and disease again. Through the sacrifice of Jesus, my sin and its penalty have been washed away forever. I loose myself from sin consciousness through the power of Your blood and the authority of Your Word. I command all lying thoughts, emotions, and physical symptoms to cease and desist in Jesus's name. Father, I now declare that I am forgiven. I am free to worship You in spirit and in truth. I do not have to earn my healing, but it is fully paid for and complete. Thank You, Lord, for Your love for me. I am the healed of the Lord, in Jesus's name. Amen!

Day 3

POWER IN THE BLOOD

Whom God hath set forth to be a propitiation through faith in His blood, to declare His righteousness for the remission of sins that are past, through the forbearance of God. —Romans 3:25

Have you ever had an article of clothing that was so filthy, so deeply soiled, that you felt you had to throw it away? Before you discarded the garment, you probably tried your best to remove its stains. This usually calls for some very powerful cleaner. You may even need to soak it overnight. Sometimes, even after you've soaked it and washed it, there is still a residue of the stain left on the clothing. Likewise, before we came to faith in Christ, our souls were deeply soiled. For this filthy stain, even the most powerful bleach was rendered ineffective. The only substance that could remove this blemish was the eternal blood of Jesus Christ. His blood is the only blood that can take our deepest depravity, our darkest secrets, and cleanse them white as snow, without any residue left over. There is power in the blood of Jesus. In fact, the Bible says that the life of the flesh is contained in the blood (see Leviticus 17:11). Jesus's blood not only cleanses us from sin but gives us eternal life. Whatever we apply the blood to is cleansed and made alive. Therefore, when you or someone you love faces sickness or the symptoms thereof, apply the blood to it. Declare that whatever you are facing is powerless against the blood of the Lamb. Just like your sin-sick soul was cleansed by the precious blood of Jesus, that same blood cleanses your body of sickness, disease, cancer, leukemia, lupus, or any other disease of the blood or flesh. The blood of Jesus heals you now!

HEALING PRAYER

Father, in the name of Jesus Christ, I thank You for the precious blood of the Lamb Jesus, which washes away sin and infirmity from my spirit, soul, and body. I thank You that the zoe life of God is contained within the blood of Jesus, and that blood gives life, health, and strength to my body and soul. I command all feelings of guilt, condemnation, and inadequacy to be washed away with Your precious blood. I declare that every part of my being is covered by and saturated in the blood of Jesus. I specifically command cancer, growths, tumors, and any other illegal agent in my body to be destroyed by the power of Jesus. In Jesus's name I ask these things, amen!

CHRIST OUR RIGHTEOUSNESS

HEALING MEDITATION

For if by one man's offence death reigned by one; much more they which receive abundance of grace and of the gift of righteousness shall reign in life by one, Jesus Christ. —Romans 5:17

What is righteousness? The simplest way to define it would be a position of right standing with God. To illustrate this truth, recall the story of Noah and the Ark. God told Noah to build an ark, which would be occupied by his family and two of every animal that God chose. As long as Noah and the other occupants of the ark stayed within, they would be protected from the wrath of God in the form of a great flood. This is essentially what righteousness is. It is a right position in God whereby He favors us. Romans 5:17 tells us that we have been given the gift of righteousness. This righteousness means that God sees us through the lenses of His Son Jesus Christ. There is nothing you and I can do to earn it; we have it by virtue of the finished work of Christ. In fact, by faith we have received the very righteousness of Christ Himself. So the next time you look in the mirror, remember that you possess the righteousness of Christ. Satan no longer has the legal right to afflict you any longer. Now that you are in right standing with God through the blood of Jesus, you have legal grounds to tell sickness, disease, and affliction to leave your body for good. No matter what you are facing or what you are going through, be encouraged today. Because you have received the gift of Christ's righteousness, you can rule and reign as a king in life. Stand up and take your place in God. Nothing can hold you in captivity any longer.

HEALING PRAYER

Father, in the name of Jesus Christ, I thank You for who You are and all that You have done in my life. I believe that Jesus Christ was the propitiatory sacrifice for my sin, and that through His blood I have been made righteous. I thank You, Father, that I have the very righteousness of Christ. It is Your eternal gift to me. Through this gift of righteousness, I reign in life. Therefore, sickness, disease, affliction, infirmity, and oppression of all forms must leave my body now. I take authority over the power of Satan and I declare that he is defeated. I am no longer a victim of my circumstances, but I live in victory over them. I possess the promise of healing and deliverance right now in Jesus's name. No lying symptom or pain will control my mind or body any longer. In the name of Jesus I am healed!

Day 5

ALL MANNER OF SICKNESS MUST GO

HEALING MEDITATION

And Jesus went about all Galilee, teaching in their synagogues, and preaching the gospel of the kingdom, and healing all manner of sickness and all manner of disease among the people. —Matthew 4:23

I recently went to visit one of my favorite retail stores. When I arrived at the entrance of the store, there was a plastered wall covering the front of it. I was shocked! I noticed a young lady standing by the entrance, so I asked her, "Where did they go?" She replied, "They went out of business." Still in disbelief,

I walked around to the side of the store to peak through the window. As I gazed inside, there were liquidation signs with the phrase, *everything must go*. What happened? For various reasons, this store closed down and went through liquidation. Liquidation is defined as the termination of a business operation and the discharging of its liabilities. Two thousand years ago, Jesus came to destroy the works of Satan (see 1 John 3:8). The word *works* is the Greek word *ergon*, meaning business operations (Strong's, G2041). Every residue of the curse that was introduced through Adam was removed through the atoning work of the Son of God. Jesus put Satan out of business. What was Satan's business? Oppression, bondage, sickness, and disease. Jesus went all throughout Galilee teaching and healing "*all* manner of sickness." There was nothing His healing power could not address. Whether it was cancer, diabetes, MS, lupus, blindness, AIDS, or arthritis, nothing could hinder His power to heal. In Matthew 10:1 Jesus turned around and gave His disciples the power to do the same thing He had been doing. Therefore, it is time for you to discharge the liabilities (sickness) in your life. It is time to liquidate Satan's inventory. It is time to serve notice to the devil—*all manner of sickness must go!*

HEALING PRAYER

Father, in the name of Jesus, I thank You that through the cross of Christ You have destroyed the works of the devil according to 1 John 3:8. I declare that the works of the devil are no longer operational in my life. I decree that all manner of sickness and all manner of disease must leave me now. I recognize that Jesus is my Healer and He has empowered me to walk in divine health and victory in every area of my life—spirit, soul, and body. Today I serve notice to the enemy that he must go now! No sickness is allowed to operate in my soul or body from this day forward. Cancer, diabetes, lupus, MS, stroke, hypertension, infection, and any other symptom, disease, or aliment leaves me now in Jesus's name! I have the same authority in me now that Jesus had when He walked the earth; I am seated with Him in heavenly places. Thank You, Lord Jesus, for the victory over all manner of disease! In Jesus's name I pray, amen.

PEACE, BE STILL

HEALING MEDITATION

*And He arose, and rebuked the wind, and said
unto the sea, Peace, be still. And the wind ceased,
and there was a great calm.* —Mark 4:39

We all have had our share of storms in our life—
maybe some of us more than others. What makes
a storm a storm and how should we respond to them when
they occur? As a kid I remember intense lightning storms
raging near our house. Sometimes we would turn off all
the electricity in the house and wait patiently for it to pass.
Life can be like this sometimes. We face challenges in our
family, health, or finances, and like the disciples we ask

Jesus, "Where are You? Don't You care if we perish?" Jesus responded to this question by declaring, "Peace, be still." What a response. If Jesus is truly our Master, and we are to follow in His steps, then it only stands to reason that He was doing more than simply addressing the disciples' peril. He was actually giving every disciple throughout time a pattern of what to do when we face storms. We are to rebuke them and command peace in the midst of the situation. Jesus never became a victim of His storm, but a master over it. In fact, the storm was never designed to put the disciples in peril, but to test their faith. Notice I did not say it was to test their character. God does not use circumstances to test us, but He takes advantage of every challenge in our lives to strengthen our faith in Him. Why did Jesus rebuke the wind? The winds had become violent; they were now a threat to the disciples' well-being. Jesus put the storm in its proper context. He essentially declared to the storm, "Enough is enough!" I don't know what you are facing today, but you have been given authority by God to command the peace of God to invade your situation. Peace, be still!

HEALING PRAYER

Father, in the name of Jesus, I thank You for who You are and all that You have done. I am so grateful that You are with me in the midst of the storms of life. I recognize that nothing I am going through now is for my peril but for the development of my faith. I declare peace to this storm, sickness, disease, or infirmity. I recognize that Your Word is true and unfailing. I will not fear destruction, calamity, or death in the midst of my storm, but I will stand boldly in faith as a master of my circumstances. I take control of my emotions through the power of Your Word. I dwell in complete safety in Your presence. I command the raging of this storm to cease and for every dimension of my life to come into divine order. I know You are with me and everything You have ordained for my life will come into full manifestation. I know I am healed and whole because Your Word says I am. I pray all of these things in Jesus's name. Amen.

Day 7

NO WEAPON SHALL PROSPER

HEALING MEDITATION

No weapon that is formed against thee shall prosper; and every tongue that shall rise against thee in judgment thou shalt condemn. This is the heritage of the servants of the Lord, and their righteousness is of Me, saith the Lord. —Isaiah 54:17

The enemy of our soul is always attempting to fashion weapons against us to bring us into fear, bondage, and condemnation. Do you know what the enemy's greatest weapon is? It is the power of words! Satan is a slanderer.

He uses false words to accuse and discourage the people of God. This is what the Bible means when it says that no weapon formed against us shall prosper. The devil uses evil reports and fear against the saints, but God says that it will not work. Stop listening to the lies of the enemy. Stop allowing him to whisper in your ear and tell you that God has not answered your prayer or that you deserve what is happening to you. The tongue of the enemy is condemned! This means he has been tried in the courts of heaven and found guilty. There are also grounds for God to execute His righteous judgment upon the enemy. Oftentimes we don't see the words that we hear and the thoughts in our mind as weapons, but that is exactly what they are. Second Corinthians 10:4 says, "For the weapons of our warfare are not carnal, but mighty through God to the pulling down of strong holds." Just as the enemy has weapons, so do we as born-again believers. We can cancel what the devil says by speaking faith-filled words over our body, mind, and circumstances. The devil is absolutely incapable of speaking the truth, which means everything he says is a lie. When the enemy tells you that you are sick, he is lying. When he tells you that you will never recover, it's a lie. These are simply weapons he is employing for our destruction. Learn to see them for what they are. Through the power of God's Word, we will never be victims to the lies of the devil again. He is defeated! No weapon formed against us shall prosper!

HEALING PRAYER

Father, in the name of Jesus, I thank You for Your unfailing Word. Through Your Word I have the victory over the weapons of the enemy and I declare according to Isaiah 54:17 that no weapon formed against me shall prosper. The enemy is defeated through the power of the Word of God. I refuse to bow to any evil report. I refuse to be afraid. I reject every lie of the evil one in the name of Jesus. I am the righteousness of God in Christ, and I do not deserve sickness, disease, infirmity, or defeat. I speak life over my situation right now. I declare divine healing and wholeness over every area of my life. By faith I condemn the slanderous tongue of the devil. He is a liar, and everything he says and does is rooted in deception. Thank You, Lord, that nothing the enemy does has power to hurt me, but I have been given supernatural authority. I exercise Your authority now by declaring that this situation and/ or circumstance shall turn out for my good and for Your glory, in Jesus's name. Amen!

JESUS: YOUR GREAT PHYSICIAN

HEALING MEDITATION

When the even was come, they brought unto Him many that were possessed with devils: and He cast out the spirits with His word, and healed all that were sick: that it might be fulfilled which was spoken by Esaias the prophet, saying, Himself took our infirmities, and bare our sicknesses. —Matthew 8:16-17

In the book of Exodus, God told the Israelites that if they would hearken to His commands, He would put none of the diseases upon them that He placed upon the Egyptians, for He was the God "that healeth thee" (Exodus 15:26). This expression is a compound word in the Hebrew language, *Jehovah Rapha* or *Jehovah Ropheka*, which means the "Great Physician" (Strong's, H3068, H7495). Simply put, God is our Healer. He knows exactly what it is we need and He supplies our need according to His Word. Not only did He heal the Israelites of old, but Jesus Christ came two thousand years ago to manifest Himself on our behalf as the Healer. Jesus Christ healed all the people that were brought to Him; this was not only an act of love and compassion, but it was a fulfillment of Isaiah 54. If Jesus is the Great Physician, then there is nothing you are facing in your body today that He is not able and willing to heal. Don't be discouraged by whatever you are facing in your physical body; it is no match for the sovereign power of God. There is no sickness or disease that can stand before our Great Physician. He longs to heal you and deliver you because that is who He is. Healing is God's nature. He heals us because He loves us, and He wants us to fulfill our divine purpose in the earth. There are no limits or restrictions on His healing power. Jesus bore our sins and carried our diseases so we no longer need to bare them. Whether it is cancer, diabetes, heart disease, arthritis, kidney disease, infection, or any other ailment for that matter, it does not make any difference to God. He wants you whole! Through His power you can be healed. By faith you will stand victorious over the physical pain and infirmity in your body, and you will testify of the goodness of God in your life. Jesus is your Great Physician.

HEALING PRAYER

Father, in the name of Jesus, I thank You for Your goodness. Lord, I recognize that You are the Great Physician and I acknowledge You as my personal Healer. I believe Your Word, and I declare in faith that there is nothing impossible for You. There is no sickness or disease You cannot heal. Thank You, Lord, for healing me now! Through the blood of Jesus, I am a covenant child of God; therefore, I declare that the promise of divine healing is mine to enjoy. I command all lying symptoms in my body to cease and desist. I accept Your provision of healing as an act of Your great love for me as Your child. I receive Your healing power into my very being now. Sickness cannot stay in my body any longer because the Greater One lives inside of me, and He heals all of my diseases. Healing is my covenant right, and I insist upon my right to be healed in Jesus's name. Thank You, Lord, that I am completely made whole in You. In Your name I pray, amen.

Day 9

HEALED BY HIS STRIPES

HEALING MEDITATION

*Who His own self bare our sins in His own
body on the tree, that we, being dead to sins,
should live unto righteousness: by whose
stripes ye were healed.* —1 Peter 2:24

What did Jesus come to do? In the book of Isaiah,
the Bible prophesied the coming Messiah and His
prophetic assignment (see Isaiah 54)—He would bear our
sins and carry our diseases. This is exactly what Jesus did.
What does it mean that He bore our sins? The word *bear*
in the Greek means to place upon oneself anything as a
load to be carried. Jesus took our sickness and disease as a

load upon Himself. The question is: If He bore them, then why do you still need to bear them? The answer is that you don't any longer! Jesus bore the heaviest burden in the universe—the sins of all humanity. In perfect obedience to the Father, our Lord took upon Himself the penalty of our sins and iniquities. God nailed them to the cross of Christ and washed them away in His own blood. This sacrifice not only addressed man's depravity, but it also fully addressed the by-product of man's sin, which was sickness, poverty, and even death itself. Jesus carried it all! The curse was broken. In the book of Galatians, the Bible says, "Christ hath redeemed us from the curse of the law, being made a curse for us: for it is written, Cursed is every one that hangeth on a tree" (3:13). Every stripe on the back of Jesus categorically removed sickness from the bodies of born-again believers. That includes you and me! Now that you are saved, you no longer have to tolerate the affliction of the enemy on your body. It does not matter what you are dealing with today, Jesus paid a tremendous price for your healing and He intends for you to walk in health. The word *healed* in 1 Peter 2:24 means that you were cured or made whole. This healing has already taken place; it already belongs to you. Take possession of your healing today!

HEALING PRAYER

Father, in the name of Jesus, I thank You for sending Your Son Jesus Christ to die on the cross for my sins. Lord, I am grateful that You took upon Yourself my sicknesses and diseases. I recognize that because You bore my diseases, I no longer have to bear them. Through the stripes of Jesus Christ I am healed and made whole from every sickness, disease, infirmity, and ailment in my body and in my emotions. I declare that I am whole, from the crown of my head to the very soles of my feet; every part of my being is made whole by Your blood. I stand encouraged and empowered through the knowledge of Your Word, which tells me that I was healed. I am not waiting on You to heal me, but I am declaring in faith that I am already healed because You paid the ultimate price two thousand years ago. From this day forward I stand in confidence and assurance that You are my Healer. Nothing Satan throws my way can prevent me from walking in Your perfect will for my life, which is divine health and wholeness. I receive my healing now, in Jesus's name. Amen!

Day 10

DON'T PRAY AND WORRY

HEALING MEDITATION

Therefore I say unto you, What things soever ye desire, when ye pray, believe that ye receive them, and ye shall have them. —Mark 11:24

Prayer is a very powerful tool God has given us to invite His divine intervention into the affairs of life. It is also a powerful weapon to be used against sickness and disease. However, many people don't understand prayer. When I was a young man, I can remember praying a prayer something like this: "Now I lay me down to sleep," or "God, help!" Prayer is much more than begging for help, and it is greater than the religious exercises we have been taught.

Prayer actually works. It brings about change in our lives supernaturally. The Bible says that we are to believe that we receive *when* we pray, not *if* we pray (see Mark 11:24). As believers, we have been called to pray without ceasing (see 1 Thessalonians 5:17). The question is: What is the posture we should assume in prayer? The Word of God says we should believe we receive what we ask from Him. The word *receive* in the passage is the word *lambano*, and it means "to take to one's self, to claim, *to take a thing due*" (Strong's, G2983). This means that when we pray, we should have an attitude of possession. We must believe by faith that we have already received what we asked for. In other words, you shouldn't pray and worry. Worrying is the fastest way to neutralize answered prayer. When we worry, we are telling God He can't do what He says He will do. The attitude we have when we pray will determine our ability to receive the answer to that prayer. Are you dealing with sickness, disease, or infirmity? Once you ask God to heal you, simply thank Him for the healing He has already given you. It is yours in Christ! Whether you can see it or not makes no difference. The moment you pray, you must take ownership of the miracle for which you are asking. The Bible commands us to take no thought for our lives. So why are you worried? What will worry produce except anxiety and frustration? Your prayers have already been answered. Your miracle is in the process of manifesting. Simply believe!

HEALING PRAYER

Father, thank You for the supernatural power of prayer. Through communion with You, I now receive my miracle by faith in Your Word. I know Your Word is true, and I know that the prayer of faith will bring deliverance in my life according to James 5. I refuse to worry from this day forward. I command all fear, anxiety, stress, and doubt to leave my mind. In the name of Jesus, I declare that I rest in faith and trust in the integrity of Your Word. The moment I prayed, my prayer was answered. Thank You for the answer to my supplication. I now take possession of my healing, deliverance, and breakthrough. Healing is mine! I refuse to be manipulated by the severity of my condition, but instead I choose to rejoice in Your great power and ability to bring Your Word to pass in my life, in Jesus's name, amen.

Day 11

SPEAK TO THE MOUNTAIN...

For verily I say unto you, That whosoever shall say unto this mountain, Be thou removed, and be thou cast into the sea; and shall not doubt in his heart, but shall believe that those things which he saith shall come to pass; he shall have whatsoever he saith. —Mark 11:23

Have you ever thought about the part you play in your own healing? What did Jesus mean when He said, "Whosoever shall say unto this mountain, Be thou removed.... He shall have whatsoever he saith"? Beloved, this is the power of the spoken Word. The truth of the matter is that you and I have to participate with God in order to receive and keep our healing. God does not need our help, but He requires our participation. Most people were raised to believe that God does all the work and they are not required to do anything. As a result, people pray, "God, heal me!" and when they don't see anything happen, they automatically assume it wasn't His will to heal them. The reality is that we have to come to a place where we are doing more than just praying; we have to speak to the mountain of sickness. When Jesus said that whoever "shall say," He was using the Greek word *eipon*, which at its root means to declare (Strong's, G2036). A declaration is a formal or explicit statement or announcement, usually with the notion of authority. We are to declare to our body that it is healed; we are to declare to our mind that it is restored. God never said that we should pray about mountains; He said we should speak to them in faith and with authority. So no matter what you are facing today, open your mouth and make some declarations according to the Word of God. Speak to cancer and tell it to be removed. Speak to diabetes and tell it to go! You will have what you say. Remember to never negotiate with that mountain (whatever it may be), but stand your ground and prophetically declare your victory.

HEALING PRAYER

Father, in the name of Jesus Christ, I declare that Your Word is the final authority in my life. Right now, I decree by faith that the mountain of sickness in all of its forms and manifestations is removed from me. I exercise the divine authority You gave me in Christ. Every fear, pain, discouragement, struggle, difficulty, bondage, and infirmity must leave my body and soul now in Jesus's name. I speak to all lying symptoms affecting my mind or body— they must cease. Lord Jesus, thank You for being my Healer as well as my Redeemer. According to Mark 11:23, I speak faith-filled words and refuse to doubt in my heart that what I say, based on Your Word, shall come to pass. I am not intimidated by what I see, hear, or feel; I am convinced by Your Word and I stand on it in faith and obedience. I declare that I am healed from the crown of my head to the very soles of my feet. I speak my miracle into being right now. Nothing is impossible to me because I am a believer in Your holy Word. In Jesus's name I pray, amen.

NO MORE PAIN

HEALING MEDITATION

*Look upon mine affliction and my pain;
and forgive all my sins. O keep my soul, and
deliver me: let me not be ashamed; for I put
my trust in Thee. —Psalm 25:18,20*

No one likes pain. In fact, this is one of the reasons why sickness is so difficult to bear, because it can be extremely painful. Pain is our body's way of telling us that something is wrong. When you are in bed late at night and a pain grips your body, it can be devastating. On the other hand, you may have received a diagnosis of cancer and you are currently enduring the pain in your body partly due to treatment and therapy. Satan knows pain is very difficult for human beings to deal with and he uses this physical reality as an attempt to manipulate and control us. The really good news is that God knows what we are facing more than any one else does, and He has made provision in His Word to deal with pain. David said in Psalm 25, "Look upon my affliction and my pain." The word *affliction* means misery and trouble. David cried out to God to remove the pain of his struggle. The implication is that God does not want us to be in misery and pain, but He wants us to be well. Jesus not only paid the price for our sins and sicknesses, but He took upon Himself the pain associated with those diseases. God has given us power over the pain. Just as mountains of sickness can be removed by speaking to them, so pain can be removed by speaking to our bodies what the Word of God says. Whenever you feel pain, speak life to your body and declare that you are pain free, because God delivers you out of all your afflictions.

HEALING PRAYER

Father, in Jesus's name, I thank You that You are the God of all comfort, who brings comfort to every area of my life. According to 2 Corinthians 1:3-4, "Blessed be God, even the Father of our Lord Jesus Christ, the Father of mercies, and the God of all comfort; Who comforteth me in all our tribulation, that we may be able to comfort them which are in any trouble, by the comfort wherewith we ourselves are comforted of God." Holy Spirit, I invite Your presence into every area of my life and physical body to manifest Your supernatural power. In the name of Jesus I ask all of this, amen.

HEALTH TO YOUR FLESH

HEALING MEDITATION

For they are life unto those that find them, and health to all their flesh. —Proverbs 4:22

I n the book of Proverbs, the writer states that we should attend to his words. What words are being referred to? This is the Hebrew word *dabar*, and it refers to speech, utterance, or a command (Strong's, H1696). The Word of God is His instruction and commands for our life. This Word is alive and active, and the more we ingest it, the more it becomes health to our flesh. So many times we feel helpless against the things we face physically, emotionally, or spiritually, but the truth is that the Word of God has the power to manifest health and wholeness in every part of our being. The amazing part of this Scripture is that it refers specifically to our flesh. Just as physical food is absolutely necessary to have a healthy body, the Word of God is absolutely necessary for the health and vibrancy of our total man, especially our physical body. There is a saying, "You are what you eat." And this saying is absolutely true. Sometimes Scripture is the last thing we think about when we hear an evil report from the doctor, but the reality is that it is the most important thing we can take advantage of in those moments. Whether it is a skin disease, a bodily infection, or any other physical symptom in your body, open your mouth and declare that the Word of God is health to all your flesh. Doing this in faith will activate God's supernatural power in your very being.

HEALING PRAYER

Father, in Jesus's name, I thank You that Your Word has the power to manifest health and wholeness in my total man. Thank You, Lord Jesus, for being health to my flesh as the living Word of God. Every time I meditate on and speak Your Word, it quickens my physical body. No disease or infirmity can withstand the power of the Word of God. I command every contrary thing in my mind, body, or soul to be uprooted and consumed by the fire of the Holy Spirit. Just as children eat food to grow strong and healthy, I now open my spirit to the Word in order to receive supernatural strength and healing in Jesus's name. Amen!

A BALM IN GILEAD

HEALING MEDITATION

*Is there no balm in Gilead; is there no physician
there? why then is not the health of the daughter
of My people recovered?* —Jeremiah 8:22

In ancient Israel there were people called apothecaries, and their responsibility was to concoct ointments and salves for medicinal purposes. One of these ointments was the famous balm of Gilead. This particular balm was made from the resin of a plant that grew in Gilead, a mountainous area east of the Jordan River. It was widely popular for its healing properties. In the book of Jeremiah, the Lord asked Israel a rhetorical question, "Is there no balm in

Gilead; is there no physician there?" The obvious answer to this question is yes. There is a balm in Gilead, and that balm is the Lord Jesus Himself. He is the healing salve who takes away all of our diseases. I remember when I was a little boy, my mother would put menthol and eucalyptus on my chest when I had congestion or a cold. The fumes from that ointment would go deep down into my nasal passages and bring refreshing and healing. The Word of God works in much the same way! The question remains: If there is a balm available to the people of God, then why are God's people still suffering needlessly? Many are not applying this supernatural balm to their mind, body, and soul. The Bible tells us that Jesus is the Word, and when we meditate upon the Word of God, it brings health and healing to every part of our being. There is a balm in Gilead! You can apply the supernatural salve of the Word right now. Be encouraged today, because there is nothing that God's Word cannot heal. Receive your miracle in the name of Jesus!

HEALING PRAYER

Father, in the name of Jesus, I thank You that Your Word is the healing ointment that heals my soul and body. I declare that I no longer have to live under the power of sickness and disease because You are my balm in Gilead. Lord, You are my Great Physician. By faith I apply the Word of God to every pain, heartache, physical ailment, and emotional distress. As my Great Physician, I yield to Your healing power. According to Proverbs 4:22, Your Word is health to my flesh. I am the healed of the Lord in every area of my life. I command every symptom of sickness and disease to leave me now. I receive Your supernatural wholeness in my body so that I can fulfill my divine purpose on the earth. With long life I will be satisfied and the length of my days shall be fulfilled. Thank You, Father, for health and healing.

Day 15

GOD'S UNFAILING WORD

HEALING MEDITATION

So shall My word be that goeth forth out of My mouth: it shall not return unto Me void, but it shall accomplish that which I please, and it shall prosper in the thing whereto I sent it. —Isaiah 55:11

"In the beginning was the Word, and the Word was with God, and the Word was God" (John 1:1). If you haven't realized by now, you should know that the Word of God is the most powerful thing there is. Many people neglect to acknowledge the Word's power. The reality is that the Word of God contains the unlimited power of God; there is nothing in your life that the Word of God cannot transform. In fact, God is so convinced of the power of His Word that He says it will not return to Him void. The Hebrew word for *void* is *reyqam*, and it means "empty, vain, or without effect" (Strong's, H7387). The Word of God will never be without effect in your life; it will never fail to complete its mission. Every time you consciously proclaim the Word of God in faith, it releases the supernatural power of heaven. The challenge is a little thing called time. In the realm of the natural, we are confined to time. The Word of God is eternal and is not confined by time or space; therefore, the moment we read, speak, and obey it, the Word begins to move mightily on our behalf. Time is not a factor! God says that His Word will accomplish what He pleases. That is to say, His Word will accomplish His will. When you find yourself battling a physical condition, declare the promises of God's Word over your life with the conviction that what you are speaking will produce exactly what it says. When God speaks to you and says that you are healed, He knows that the promise of healing is destined to bring health and wholeness to your body. Keep standing on the Word of God, no matter your circumstances. Don't allow the devil to deceive you into believing that God's Word has no effect—the Word will never fail!

HEALING PRAYER

Father, I thank You for Your unfailing Word. In the name of Jesus Christ, I declare that no promise from Your Word spoken in my life shall return void. The words I speak over myself in faith and in agreement with Your Word shall not fall to the ground. Every purpose that You intend in my life shall be accomplished. Thank You that Your Word is full of omnipotent power, and any barrier to its fulfillment in my life is broken now. Nothing will stand in the way of me receiving the manifestation of Your promises in my life. I know Satan is a liar, and I reject his lies as an act of my free will. Thank You, Lord, that Your Word is prosperous in my life. Your Word says, according to 1 Peter 2:24, that with the stripes of Jesus I was already healed. This Word is the final authority in my life. I decree divine health, wholeness, restoration, and deliverance in my spirit, soul, and body, in Jesus's name. Amen!

WHAT YOU SAY IS WHAT YOU GET!

HEALING MEDITATION

*Thou shalt also decree a thing, and it shall
be established unto thee: and the light shall
shine upon thy ways.* —Job 22:28

Nothing, in my opinion, has been more underesti-
mated than the power of our words. God made us in
His image and after His likeness (see Genesis 1:26-28), and
He gave us the ability to speak things that either create or
destroy. Life and death are in the power of your tongue
(see Proverbs 18:21). This is a spiritual reality you cannot

afford to neglect. What are you speaking on a daily basis? Are you speaking life or are you speaking death? This is the responsibility of each individual believer. The Bible says that we shall decree a thing and it shall be established. The word *decree* in this passage is *gazar*, and it means "to divide or cut off" (Strong's, H1504). Our words are like demarcation lines in the spiritual realm. What we say determines what we will accept and what we will not tolerate. If you say you are the healed of the Lord, then it becomes difficult for you to accept sickness. Why? Because a line in the sand has been drawn through the words you have spoken. What you speak or decree will be "established," which is the Hebrew word *quwm*, and it means "to rise or stand" (Strong's, H6965). In other words, what you say will stand. Many times we blame God for what "He allows," but the reality is that we have been given authority in the earth to make decrees and see these decrees come to fruition. Simply put, what you say is what you get! What are you saying today? Are you decreeing God's promise of healing and wholeness over your life? It is not too late to change what you decree; you can start right now! Never forget that your words have power. Don't allow Satan to take advantage of you. Stop letting him inflict you with sickness and disease. Make some faith decrees today. You are the head and not the tail, above only and not beneath (see Deuteronomy 28:13). Rise up and be blessed!

HEALING PRAYER

Father, in the name of Jesus, I thank You for who You are and all that You have done. Right now, I decree and declare that I walk in divine health. I am 100 percent healthy in Jesus's name. Lord, Your Word says in 1 Peter 2:24 that with the stripes of Jesus I was healed; therefore, I declare that I am healed. Every cell in my body must bow down to the lordship of Jesus Christ. I command all lying symptoms to cease immediately in Jesus's name. My body is the temple of the Holy Ghost. Sickness cannot dwell in this temple. I walk in total victory over sickness and disease in Jesus's name. According to Job 22:28, what I decree in faith shall be established. My healing is through the shed blood of Jesus, so I declare that no sickness, disease, infirmity, or unclean spirit can remain in my body. Amen!

Day 17

MEDITATE DAY AND NIGHT

HEALING MEDITATION

*This book of the law shall not depart out of
thy mouth; but thou shalt meditate therein
day and night, that thou mayest observe to do
according to all that is written therein: for then
thou shalt make thy way prosperous, and then
thou shalt have good success.* —Joshua 1:8

As a young believer in Jesus, I was blessed to adopt the
habit of regular Bible study and Scripture meditation.
In fact, I would read and quote the Bible all day long. Little
did I know that I was unleashing supernatural power in my
life. The Bible tells us in Joshua 1:8, "This book of the law
shall not depart out of thy mouth; but thou shalt meditate

therein day and night." What does it mean to meditate in the law day and night? The word *law* is the word *torah*, and it simply means the Word of God (Strong's, H8451). The word *meditate* comes from the Hebrew word *hagah*, and it means "to moan, growl, utter, or mutter" (Strong's, H1904). Simply put, meditation on the Word of God means to speak it over and over again to yourself. This is not the same as Eastern meditation; it is not entering into some sort of trance, but it is simply affirming the Word of God in your personal time of devotion. It is like a cow chewing cud; he chews then regurgitates, then chews again. This process helps us to internalize the promises of God for our own lives. By speaking the Word consistently to yourself, you are building up your spirit man in faith. Whatever the area of need in your life may be, meditate on the Word of God in that area. For instance, if you are dealing with the symptoms of sickness or infirmity, speak the promises of God concerning healing over and over to yourself until it becomes alive and active on the inside of you. The voice in your life that speaks the loudest is the voice you will heed. This is a very simple yet profound spiritual principle. And it is why you have to be intentional about what you are allowing into your ear gates. Take some time today to meditate on God's Word. Speak to yourself that you are the healed of the Lord according to Exodus 15:26 and 1 Peter 2:24. Say it over and over again until it "clicks." This is how you are going to defeat sickness and disease in your life, by speaking louder and more frequently than the problem. Today is your day!

HEALING PRAYER

Father, in the name of Jesus, I thank You that Your Word is the final authority in my life. The Bible tells me to meditate on Your Word day and night, and by faith I am committed to obeying this instruction. I am a believer in Your Word and I now declare that the Word of God is more powerful than any situation I may face. As I speak Your Word in faith, I know that sickness, disease, and infirmity are being dissolved by the supernatural power of God. I drive out everything and anything that is not like You through muttering and speaking Your Word consistently. I recognize I am more than a conqueror through You. I declare that greater is He that lives within me than He that is in the world. Nothing is impossible to me because I believe Your Word without doubt or reservation. Now Father, I thank You that You are working in me to both will and to do Your good pleasure according to Philippians 2:13. In Jesus's name I pray, amen!

THE CHILDREN'S BREAD

HEALING MEDITATION

*But Jesus said unto her, Let the children first
be filled: for it is not meet to take the children's
bread, and to cast it unto the dogs.* —Mark 7:27

In the book of Mark, the Bible tells a powerful story:
"For a certain woman, whose young daughter had an
unclean spirit, heard of Him, and came and fell at His feet:
the woman was a Greek, a Syrophenician by nation; and
she besought Him that He would cast forth the devil out
of her daughter. But Jesus said unto her, Let the children
first be filled: for it is not meet to take the children's bread,
and to cast it unto the dogs. And she answered and said

unto Him, Yes, Lord: yet the dogs under the table eat of the children's crumbs" (Mark 7:25-28). As you can see, this Syrophenician woman was in a very desperate situation. Her daughter was being afflicted. To this request Jesus responded by telling her that what she was requesting is the "children's bread." What does that mean? It means that healing is a benefit of being in covenant relationship with God. It means that God's children are entitled to it. The word *bread* simply means food or sustenance. Just as a baby is entitled to his mother's breast milk, so we, the children of God, are entitled to divine healing. It is not a matter of if God wills it; it is a matter of if we will receive it. God said that He would put none of the diseases on the children of Israel that He placed on the Egyptians (see Exodus 15:26). This is a promise that distinguishes the children of covenant and those who don't have a covenant with God—healing belongs to the New Covenant believer in Jesus Christ. All you and I have to do is place a demand on it by faith, and God will show Himself to be *El Shaddai*, our all-sufficient source of the "children's bread."

HEALING PRAYER

Father, in the precious name of Your Son Jesus, I thank You that healing is the "children's bread." Through the blood of Jesus Christ, I have been given access to the promise of healing, and I recognize that healing is mine to enjoy. Thank You, Lord, for being the God that heals all of my diseases. I am not moved by what I see or feel, but I am only moved by the unadulterated Word of God. I am fully persuaded that You are the only Healer. Jesus Christ bore my sicknesses and carried my diseases on the cross, and because of that biblical truth, healing is the divine right of every born-again believer. I declare that I walk in divine health because the supernatural promises of the Word of God are working in me right now. I am full of the children's bread in body, soul, and spirit. In the name of Your Son I pray, amen!

Day 19

BE STRONG AND VERY COURAGEOUS

HEALING MEDITATION

Only be thou strong and very courageous, that thou mayest observe to do according to all the law, which Moses My servant commanded thee: turn not from it to the right hand or to the left, that thou mayest prosper whithersoever thou goest. —Joshua 1:7

Courage is a very powerful attribute. Have you ever been afraid to move forward? Have you ever questioned the outcome of a situation or circumstance? This is when we need courage the most. *Webster's Dictionary* defines courage as strength in the face of pain or grief. It is the ability to act when fear is present. God told Joshua, "Be thou strong and very courageous." Why did He tell him this? The Israelites were about to enter into the Promised Land; they were about to experience their prophetic destiny. It is in the times we are closest to the breakthrough that we need the most courage. *Courage* comes from the Hebrew word *'amats*, meaning to be strong, bold, and solid (Strong's, H553). This is what God is saying to you today beloved—be strong! Don't allow the pain in your body or the symptoms of your ailment to discourage you from walking into the promise of healing and wholeness. There may be some things you are facing today that look like giants, but remember, "The Lord thy God is with thee whithersoever thou goest" (Joshua 1:9). You will overcome! The key is courage. Satan will try to intimidate and deceive you, but it is just the tactic of someone who knows that he is already defeated. You will walk in divine health. You will prosper. It doesn't matter how things seem now, the Word of God cannot lie. Be strong and very courageous, beloved. Your promise is nearer than you have realized.

HEALING PRAYER

Father, in the name of Jesus, I thank You that You are the source of my strength and courage. I declare that I am very strong and courageous in You. Through the authority of Your Word I command fear, worry, and anxiety to release their hold on my mind, will, and emotions. From this day forward I walk in great boldness and authority concerning the circumstances of my life. Sickness and disease can no longer intimidate and control me. Just as the pagan nations were driven out before the nation of Israel, so I drive out sickness, disease, fear, and poverty in the name of Jesus. No weapon formed against me shall prosper. I affirm and declare that I am the head and not the tail, I am above only and not beneath, according to Deuteronomy 28:13. This is the day of victory in my life. I am healed, made whole, and restored in Jesus's name. Amen!

RIVERS OF LIVING WATER

HEALING MEDITATION

*He that believeth on Me, as the scripture
hath said, out of his belly shall flow
rivers of living water.* —John 7:38

When is the last time you've been to the river? As a kid I remember going fishing with my father. We would go on the riverbank and cast our lines all day long. I was always fascinated by the way the river flowed continuously; it almost seemed as if it never ended. Jesus said that if we would believe, out of our belly would flow rivers of living water. A river is a natural stream of water flowing in a channel to the sea or some other body of water.

So what does Jesus mean when He says that rivers of living water will flow out of our belly? Water, by nature, is life-giving. Like the natural river is a source of food and provision to the earth, so the River of Life (which is the Holy Spirit) will flow out of our innermost being and bring life to everything and everyone He encounters, including us. In the Greek, Jesus actually uses the term "torrent." This implies a violent outpouring or deluge with the power to overtake anything in its path. The truth is that the Spirit of God inside of you is a supernatural torrent that can and will overtake anything that stands in His way. When you realize that life is on the inside of you, then you will no longer tolerate sickness, poverty, and death. You are not some helpless victim of what may be happening to you, but you have a reservoir of supernatural power inside of you desperately waiting to be released. Place a demand on that river—the Holy Ghost. The Spirit of God will energize you and manifest God's healing power in your mortal flesh. How do you release this deluge? You must simply believe the Word of God. If you will believe, you will see supernatural manifestation.

HEALING PRAYER

Father, in the precious name of Jesus Christ, I thank You for the power and presence of the Holy Spirit on the inside of me. By faith in Your Word, I declare that the river within me is released. Thank You for washing away any and everything in me that is not like You. Through Your Spirit I am empowered and enabled to receive healing, health, and wholeness. There is a deluge flowing from my inner man that drives out sickness and every work of the evil one. Holy Spirit, thank You for filling me to overflowing. The life of God resonates inside of me and teaches me how to experience all things that pertain to life and godliness. I put an end to all oppression, pain, hurt, sickness, and bondage right now in the name of Jesus, and I command my healing to come forth. Greater is He that lives in me than he that is in the world. In Jesus's name I pray, amen.

YOUTH RENEWED LIKE THE EAGLES

HEALING MEDITATION

Who satisfieth thy mouth with good things; so that thy youth is renewed like the eagle's. —Psalm 103:5

The eagle is one of the most powerful birds in the bird kingdom. They are known for their swift flight, strong beak, and their extremely keen sense of sight. They are at the top of the food chain. Eagles are also known for their ability to rejuvenate themselves with the rays from the sun, which causes them to remain strong and vibrant throughout their life. The Bible says that God satisfies our mouth with good things so that our youth is renewed like the eagle's. The "good things" God is referring to is His Word. When our mouth is filled with His Word, it brings renewal to not only our spiritual man but our physical man as well. It renews our body. A healthy diet of the Word of God can ensure health to our body, because it is filled with life-giving power. Just as the rays of the sun energize the cells of the eagle and produce vibrancy in their bodies, the power of the Word rejuvenates, heals, and restores our physical being. When is the last time you thought of yourself as an eagle? Well, that is exactly what you are! Satan may be trying to convince you that you are a buzzard or a duck, but you are not. You are the head and not the tail, you are above only and not beneath. Sickness does not stand a chance against the Word of God working on the inside of you. Open up your mouth and speak life over yourself today. Confess God's Word day in and day out. As you do this, you are going to become stronger and stronger, and eventually, much like the eagle, you will soar far above everything the devil is throwing at you.

HEALING PRAYER

Father, You are the great and mighty God, and through Your Word I am empowered to prosper and live in health. Thank You, Lord, for rejuvenating me through Your Spirit and causing my youth to be renewed like the eagle's. I recognize that from this day forward I am no longer a victim of circumstances, tragedy, or illness. Your Word causes me to soar far above all affliction, pain, and defeat in my life. I am a victor through You. Lord Jesus, I am grateful for the stripes You took upon Yourself and the blood You shed for my health and wholeness. I stand confident in the power of Your Word to heal me. Just as the eagle is strong and vibrant, I am strong and resilient. I take authority over sickness, infirmity, disorder, and degeneration in my mind, body, and soul, in any form it may manifest. In Jesus's name I pray, amen!

LET THE WEAK SAY, "I AM STRONG"

HEALING MEDITATION

Beat your plowshares into swords, and your pruninghooks into spears: let the weak say, I am strong. —Joel 3:10

All of us have faced things in life that we didn't seem to have the strength to bear. For some of us, it may have come in the form of the loss of a loved one, or a problem in a relationship, or the debilitating effect of illness. No matter what it is, God's arm is not too short that He cannot save. We must realize God is aware of our struggles and He knows the limitations of our strength. It is in these moments we are to declare that we are strong despite our perceived weaknesses. The book of Joel declares, "Let the weak say, I am strong." This is a prophetic declaration that transcends both feeling and emotion. It is the choice of someone who has decided to rely on God's power and not their own. This is not just a temporary, emotional strength we obtain by deceiving ourselves into believing things aren't as bad as they seem; this is a supernatural might that God grants us by His Spirit. It is a declaration of our faith in His Word to accomplish what we cannot in our own ability. Just as God spoke to Paul, telling him, "My strength is made perfect in weakness" (2 Corinthians 12:9), so the Father is speaking to you now. It doesn't matter what the doctors have said or what your feelings are attempting to dictate, God's power is more than able to meet you at the very point of your need. Rise up out of the ashes of despair, dust yourself off, and declare, "I am strong!"

HEALING PRAYER

Father, in the name of Jesus, I thank You that Your strength is made perfect in my weakness. No matter what obstacles are before me today, I declare I am strong in You. I do not rely on natural strength, but I receive supernatural might by Your Spirit in my inward man. I recognize that Satan is defeated and that he is underneath my feet. The forces of darkness in the form of sickness, disease, and infirmity are already defeated in Jesus's name. I do not have to face any struggle in my physical power but through the power of Christ at work on the inside of me. No weapon formed against me shall prosper, and no tongue that rises against me shall go uncondemned. Thank You, Jesus, for being my Healer and my Deliverer in every area of life, especially in the physical realm. Thanks be to God who always causes me to triumph in Christ. In the matchless name of Jesus Christ I pray, amen!

Day 23

INTERNALIZE THE WORD

HEALING MEDITATION

*So then faith cometh by hearing and hearing
by the word of God.* —Romans 10:17

It is not enough to read the Bible; we must hear the revelation of the Holy Spirit from the words we read. Simply put, we must have revelation. Romans 10:17 says that faith comes by hearing and hearing comes by the Word—the *rhema*—of God. The way we obtain faith is from God's Word. The more we eat or take in the bread of the Word, the more the Holy Spirit speaks to us concerning that Word, and the more revelation we receive. This is the process in which we must internalize the Word of God. Why is internalizing it so important? The Bible says that a good man out of the good treasure of his heart brings forth good things (see Matthew 12:35). In short, you and I will bring forth what is on the inside of us, especially when pressure comes. Whatever we put inside is exactly what will come out, but only in exponential measure. If you want to overcome sickness in your life or in the life of a loved one, you must get the promises from the Word of God concerning healing deep down into your spirit. By doing this you are building your faith and causing the promises of God to become alive and active on the inside of you. Set the Word of God before your eyes day and night. Make the Word your priority. Whatever you make a priority will become your first response in times of desperation. The Word of God is full of omnipotent power that can drive out all manner of sickness and disease. Fix your eyes on God's Word and don't turn away for any reason. This is how you overcome the enemy!

HEALING PRAYER

Father, in the name of Jesus, I thank You for who You are and all that You have done. Right now, in the name of Jesus, I decree and declare that I have great faith. In accordance with Mark 11:22-23, I have the God-kind of faith and every mountain in my life and in the lives of those around me must obey my voice. I open my mouth right now and I say that doubt and unbelief must go from me. I am a believer of the Word of God. Every word in the Bible is the truth and I believe it. It is the final authority in my life. I am not moved by what I see, but I am moved by the Word of God only. I walk by faith in the Word of God and not by sight. I am not controlled by my emotions, the emotions of others, or my environment; but I am completely dominated by God's Word. In accordance with Romans 10:17, I declare that I am a hearer of Your Word and, as a result, I have great faith. Nothing is impossible to me because I am a believer of Your Word. In Jesus's name I pray. Amen.

Day 24

GOD'S POWER IN YOU!

Now unto Him that is able to do exceeding abundantly above all that we ask or think, according to the power that worketh in us. —Ephesians 3:20

Contrary to popular belief, God does not move or operate in our lives according to feelings or emotions. Does the Spirit of God evoke great emotions within us? Certainly! However, the key to being able to receive God's blessings and promises is not emotion. The truth is that your ability to experience answered prayer is contingent upon how much His power is at work on the inside of you. The word *power* used in Ephesians 3:20 is the Greek word *dynamis*, and it means explosive power or power resident in a thing by virtue of its nature (Strong's, G1411). The best way to describe this kind of power is to use the illustration of a car engine. When you stick the key in the ignition of a car, it ignites the spark plug and creates an explosion of combustible gasoline in the engine cylinder, which in turn causes the car to move. Essentially, the latent power available in the car is released. What happens when there is no gasoline in the car? The engine will stall, and no one is going anywhere. You are the engine, the Word of God is the gasoline, and faith is the ignition. The *dynamis* is the power available in the car to create motion. If we have no Word residing on the inside of us, then we will beg and scream and cry, but we, like an engine without gasoline, will see no results. Everything God does in your life is based on how much power is available in you for use. Is your tank empty or full? In order to have this power, you must deposit God's Word deep inside. This power is so great that no sickness, disease, or infirmity can stand before you. Release the supernatural power on the inside of you in order to experience healing, change, and lasting transformation today.

HEALING PRAYER

Father, I thank You that greater is He that lives in me than he that lives in the world. Right now, I receive Your dynamis power in my inner man that enables and empowers me to walk in victory and divine health. I declare that Satan is defeated. Lord, Your Word is the source of all power in my life, and I draw from that very source to meet all my needs (spirit, soul, and body). Nothing is more powerful than Your Word. I reject every excuse the enemy would give me as to why I am not living the life You have ordained for me—they are all lies. Father, I give Your Holy Spirit free reign in my life to do in me as You will and manifest the fullness of Your covenant promises in my life. I thank You, Lord, that You are able to do exceeding abundantly above all that I can dare ask or think according to Your supernatural power at work on the inside of me. These things I declare in the precious name of Your Son Jesus Christ. Amen!

Day 25

RECEIVE YOUR MIRACLE

HEALING MEDITATION

And all things, whatsoever ye shall ask in prayer,
believing, ye shall receive. —Matthew 21:22

A miracle is defined as a surprising and welcomed event that is not explicable by natural or scientific laws, and is considered to be divine. Miracles are supernatural manifestations of God's omnipotent power in the earth. To put it simply, our God is a miracle-working God. He specializes in the impossible. There is only one thing necessary when responding to a miracle—you must receive it! The Bible is filled with countless examples of ordinary people like you and me who had a supernatural encounter with God. The thing they all had in common was their willingness to receive what God wanted to do in their lives. Receiving your miracle is not passive; it must be done intentionally with faith and expectation. Don't let the enemy talk you out of your miracle. Don't waste your mental energy trying to rationalize the promises of God. The Bible says that whatever you ask in prayer, believing, you shall receive. *Receive* is the Greek word *lambano*, and it means to take a thing due (Strong's, G2983). It is an act of one who has a sense of entitlement and ownership. When something belongs to you, you simply take it! There is no need to explain or negotiate. It's yours! In the same way, it is time for you to take your miracle. Don't wait on the doctor's report or the diagnosis; receive your miracle now. Dare to take God at His Word. Whatever you have the audacity to ask for in prayer and the determination to believe, you will receive. It is that simple. What are you believing God to do today? Do you need healing in your body? Are you praying for freedom from a life-controlling addiction? Open your heart to Jesus and let Him be the miracle worker He desires to be in your life. Receive your miracle today!

HEALING PRAYER

Father, in Jesus's name, I believe that You are the Miracle Worker. Today I receive my healing miracle in all of the various areas of my life. I know deep in my heart that nothing is impossible for You. I am ready to experience Your supernatural power in my life. There is nothing that will stand in the way of me receiving my miracle. Right now, I lambano (receive) the answer to my prayer of faith and I declare that it is already done. Sickness no longer has permission to operate in my life. My body is the temple of the Holy Spirit, and I am not my own; I have been bought with a price, according to 1 Corinthians 6:20. Therefore, I glorify God in my body and in my spirit which both belong to God. No longer will I take a passive approach to the miracle I need in my life, but I will aggressively embrace what rightfully belongs to me through the shed blood of Jesus. Today is a day of total transformation and inexplicable goodness, in Jesus's name. Amen!

Day 26

"NOW" FAITH

HEALING MEDITATION

Now faith is the substance of things hoped for, the evidence of things not seen. —Hebrews 11:1

Hebrews 11:1 is one of my favorite passages in the Bible. The reason it is my favorite is primarily due to the fact that this Scripture highlights faith. Our faith in God is the basis for everything we are able to experience and receive from Him. We cannot know God without faith. We cannot please God without faith. But the question remains: If faith is so important, then why do so many Christians know so little about it? The reality is that faith (i.e., confidence or conviction) is the key ingredient to receiving your healing. This is what I call "now" faith. Incidentally, the Bible uses the primary particle "now" to bring the subject of faith into its proper context and discussion. Some believe that this was a filler inserted by the translators, but I believe it is a fascinating way of looking at the nature of faith. When we ask God for something, faith says we receive it in the present tense. In other words, faith possesses now what will be manifested in the future. What if you had the audacity to believe that you had already received your miracle, whether you can see it or not? Beloved, God has already answered your prayer! The truth is that you are already healed; just believe it and receive it! The second component of this faith is hope. Hope is a confident expectation of something good, which we await with great anticipation. Are you awaiting the manifestation of God's promise in your life with great anticipation? Today is a good day to start! Don't allow the length of your struggle to determine the level of your hope. You will see God's Word come to fruition in your life. Now is the time for you to exercise your faith.

HEALING PRAYER

Father, in Jesus's name, I thank You for the revelation of Your Word. I praise You that You have revealed to me what real faith is and how I can exercise this Bible faith to receive the miracle I need. You are an awesome God! I am convinced in my spirit that there is absolutely nothing impossible for You. Right now, I embrace supernatural hope. I confidently expect with great anticipation that You will hasten to perform Your Word in my life. I am not simply waiting on You to do something on my behalf, but I receive my breakthrough "now" by faith. Today I declare that I am healed. Everything I need is in Your Word; therefore, I speak Your Word in faith and with authority. Today is the day of my breakthrough. Through faith I embrace the promises of God for my life and possess them for my life and the lives of my loved ones. In Jesus's name I ask, amen.

Day 27

THE COVENANT OF HEALING

HEALING MEDITATION

And ye shall serve the Lord your God, and He shall bless thy bread, and thy water; and I will take sickness away from the midst of thee. There shall nothing cast their young, nor be barren, in thy land: the number of thy days I will fulfil. —Exodus 23:25-26

The truth is that you and I serve a covenant God. What does this mean? God interacts with His children on the basis of a covenant relationship. A covenant is a legal contract or agreement that confines an individual or a group of people to a certain course of action. Because God is a God of covenant, He has bound Himself to relate to us in a particular way. In Exodus 23 God reveals His covenant of healing to the Israelites. He promises He will bless their bread and water and take away sickness from among them. Did you realize that God promises to take away sickness from among His people? Why are many of God's people still sick then? The simple truth is that a covenant involves the actions of two or more parties. Though we have a covenant with God, if we are ignorant of it or don't participate in and appropriate our portion, we will not reap its benefits. The devil knows God has a covenant with you and he will attempt to do anything in his power to cut you off from that covenant. Give him no place! He is a liar! Any time sickness is operating unhindered in your life, it is violating God's covenant with you. God has obligated Himself to you as the Healer. Make no mistake about this: This covenant was ratified in full measure through the blood of Jesus. The more you meditate on the Word of God, the more you will be informed about your rights and privileges under the New Covenant. God is your Healer, and as the Healer He must heal. The truth is that you are already healed because your covenant says you are.

HEALING PRAYER

Father, in Jesus's name, I thank You for the covenant of healing You made with me as Your child. I thank You, Lord, that through the shed blood of Jesus Christ You have ratified this covenant and enforced the promise of healing in my life. You are the Healer and I acknowledge Your healing presence in my body. I stand in faith and insist upon my covenant rights according to Your Word. The Bible tells me in 1 Peter 2:24 that with the stripes of Jesus I was healed; therefore, I am the healed of the Lord. Sickness has no more permission to operate in my body illegally. I declare that it is cast out from this day forward. I declare that every lying symptom acting out in my body must cease and desist. Every cell in my body must come into alignment and obedience to the Word of God. I will no longer allow the enemy to trespass against me or oppress me physically. Today I am healed in Jesus's name. Amen!

Day 28

EMBRACING THE TRUTH

And ye shall know the truth, and the truth shall make you free. —John 8:32

Have you ever heard the expression that knowledge is power? I would say this is a gross understatement. In fact, ignorance can be detrimental to your health and well-being. If what you don't know can hurt you, then what you know can bring positive transformation to your life. Jesus said that you shall know the truth and the truth shall make you free. Oftentimes we read this Scripture out of context. We tend to think that the Scripture is saying, "And you will hear the truth and the truth will set you free." The

Bible never said that hearing the truth would set you free; rather, it says that *knowing* the truth will *make you free*— there is a difference! Knowing the truth means you are intimately acquainted with the truth. It is a Jewish idiom that signifies intercourse—Adam *knew* Eve his wife and she conceived (see Genesis 4:1). We must know the truth, for it has the power to liberate us and to make us free. Once you have been made free, it is nearly impossible to go back into captivity again. In order to know the truth, you must first embrace it. Once you embrace it, it has the permission to go deep inside your spirit and produce the fruit of freedom. Are you pregnant with the truth? Whatever you are pregnant with is what you will manifest. Become pregnant with the revelation of God's Word. Make a decision to refuse to hear anything else but what the Word says. Once the Word of God moves from your head to your heart, it will come alive inside your innermost being. Say to yourself today, "I know the truth, and the truth makes me free!"

HEALING PRAYER

Father, in Jesus's name, I praise You for Your truth. I know in my spirit that Your Word is truth. I embrace Your Word in my heart and allow it to bring revelation to my spirit. Lord Jesus, I submit to You as my Healer and Redeemer. The only thing standing between me and total victory and freedom is my willingness to receive the truth of Your Word; therefore, I declare that I know the truth and the truth makes me free according to John 8:32. Lord, I delight in Your Word; I love to meditate in Your Word all day long. Father, create in me a hunger and thirst for the truth every waking day. As I hear and meditate in Your truth, I am becoming more intimate with Jesus, and the works Jesus manifested in His life are manifested in me from this day forward. In Jesus's name I pray, amen.

Day 29

SEEING FROM GOD'S PERSPECTIVE

HEALING MEDITATION

*And Elisha prayed, and said, Lord, I pray Thee,
open his eyes, that he may see. And the Lord
opened the eyes of the young man; and he saw:
and, behold, the mountain was full of horses and
chariots of fire round about Elisha.* —2 Kings 6:17

Oftentimes we look at situations and circumstances
from a natural vantage point. We have a tendency to
look at what we can see in the physical world. There may
be an evil report issued by the doctor or a lump appearing

on some part of the body. When we look at things from this perspective, it is easy to be misled by what we see. The natural realm only represents one piece of the puzzle; unfortunately, this only accounts for a small percentage of reality. If we really want to see things the right way, we have to look from God's point of view. Elisha understood this profound truth. While being surrounded by the enemy, the prophet knew a secret his enemies did not know, namely, "they that be with us are more than they that be with them" (2 Kings 6:16). When God is with you, you are a majority! It doesn't matter what is going on around you. His servant Gehazi was so anxious about what he saw that fear took control of his mind. Surely it was over for the prophet and his servant, right? Wrong! How did Elisha respond to the situation? He prayed. This was not just any prayer; it was a prayer of faith. Elisha said, "Lord, I pray Thee, open his eyes, that he may see." The issue is not God's ability to heal, deliver, or restore; the issue is our ability to see things from God's perspective. In the spiritual realm they were surrounded with an entire host of heavenly horses, chariots, and a ring of fire. The truth is that you are surrounded as well. The angel of the Lord is surrounding you and will deliver you out of any sickness, disease, or peril you may find yourself in today. Open your eyes and see the King of kings arising with healing in His wings.

HEALING PRAYER

Father, in the name of Jesus, I thank You for opening my eyes to the reality of Your victorious kingdom. I recognize that Your Word is the final authority. It does not matter what I see in the natural realm, Your Word has the final say; through Your power I have prevailed over the enemy. I declare that there are chariots and fire surrounding me right now, so I have no fear. As I look closer at my situation, I see that You are completely in control. I command sickness and disease to go from me now in Jesus's name. I receive strength for battle in the name of Jesus. No longer will I be intimidated by what I see in the natural realm, but I will affirm the truth with bold confidence according to the Word of God. In the name of Jesus Christ I pray. Amen!

Day 30

WHAT NEXT?

HEALING MEDITATION

*Wherefore take unto you the whole armour of God,
that ye may be able to withstand in the evil day, and
having done all, to stand. Stand therefore, having
your loins girt about with truth, and having on the
breastplate of righteousness.* —Ephesians 6:13-14

There have been countless times in my life where I felt like I did not know what to do. Maybe you have felt this way as well. You may be in that place now. Have you ever said, "I have prayed, I have believed; now what?" Maybe the pain in your body or the suffering of a loved one has convinced you that God has not answered your prayer.

How are we to approach these types of situations? The Bible says that you and I are to put on the whole armor of God. Why? Because we are fighting a spiritual battle. Our walk of faith is a spiritual fight; therefore, we must gird up for the battle ahead. Notice I did not say the war, because the war has already been won through the cross of Christ. We do, however, have to engage the enemy on the battlefield of our mind. When you are praying, believing God, and not seeing the results you anticipate, the question remains: What's next? The Bible says that when you have done all to stand, stand therefore! The word *stand* in this passage is the word *histemi*, which means to remain fixed, firm, and established (Strong's, G2476). It is a position of faith and confidence. I love the fact that the Holy Spirit put the word "therefore" in the passage because it means "these things being so." What things is the Bible referring to? The promises of God's Word! The Word of God is a fixed reality. It doesn't matter how things seem; the Word will prevail in our lives. Once you realize this truth, there is only one thing left to do—stand on the Word of God. Don't allow the enemy to bully you out of your breakthrough. Do not allow time to talk you out of your confession of faith. It is already done! Stand therefore!

HEALING PRAYER

Father, in Jesus's name, I thank You that I am empowered and equipped by Your Word. Right now, I take authority over any and all discouragement, and I declare that I am strong in You and in the power of Your might. From this day forward I arm myself with the full armor of God, never to be removed again. I recognize the agenda of my enemy, and I choose to resist him steadfastly in the faith. I take the shield of faith and quench all the fiery darts of the evil one. I choose to stand, having my loins girt about with the truth. The enemy is defeated. I receive my healing and/or the healing of those for whom I am praying. No weapon formed against me will be able to prosper. I refuse to give up trusting You, God! I refuse to doubt Your Word. Thank You for the breakthrough, in Jesus's name. Amen.

Day 31

THE GARMENT OF PRAISE

To appoint unto them that mourn in Zion, to give unto them beauty for ashes, the oil of joy for mourning, the garment of praise for the spirit of heaviness; that they might be called trees of righteousness, the planting of the Lord, that He might be glorified. —Isaiah 61:3

One of the things I love about God is that He knows exactly what we are going through at all times. God is not ignorant or negligent of our pain. He is a God of love and compassion. In fact, He is in the business of lifting burdens and destroying yokes of bondage. He delights in the liberation, victory, and breakthrough of His people. This is why God hates sickness, disease, and depression as much as He does, because it brings His children into captivity. Are you burdened? Are you mourning loss? Are you experiencing depression? If you are, I have good news for you: It doesn't have to stay that way. Two thousand years ago, Jesus Christ engaged in a great exchange, a transaction that took place before all eternity. First Peter 2:24 says that Jesus bore our sins in His own body on the tree. In essence, He was taking all of our hurt, pain, and sorrow upon Himself. He exchanged our ashes for His beauty, our mourning for His joy, and He gave us the garment of praise. What is the garment of praise? It is a mantle of singing, thanksgiving, and adoration. You don't have to allow what you are facing to control your emotions. Put on the garment of praise that Jesus purchased for you by His own blood, which is a powerful weapon against the spirit of heaviness. When the devil is speaking lies in your ear, telling you what God has not done for you, drown him out by praising God. Open your mouth and begin to thank God for His goodness and merciful kindness in your life. All of a sudden, the heaviness that has been plaguing your soul will be broken.

HEALING PRAYER

Father, in Jesus's name, I thank You for giving me beauty for ashes, the oil of joy for mourning, and replacing the spirit of heaviness with the garment of praise. Thank You, Lord, that I have a reason to live and walk in Your divine purpose. I command sickness, depression, and despair to leave my body now in Jesus's name. I declare that my mouth is filled with Your wonderful works. The joy of the Lord is my strength. From this day forward I refuse to be held in captivity by the lies of the enemy. Thank You, Lord, that Your Word says I am a tree of righteousness and my life exists for Your glory. I praise You for Your merciful kindness toward me. Even now I receive my healing as I praise and worship You with my entire being. These things I ask in the matchless name of Your Son Jesus Christ. Amen!

THE LAW OF THE SPIRIT OF LIFE

HEALING MEDITATION

For the law of the Spirit of life in Christ Jesus hath made me free from the law of sin and death. —Romans 8:2

Before we were born again, we were in bondage to the world system. This included a proclivity to sin and rebellion against God, along with the accompanying curse of such rebellion, including sickness, poverty, and death. When Adam and Eve ate the fruit in the Garden of Eden, man became enslaved to his carnal nature. In fact, sickness is the direct result of man's separation from an eternal God. What was the remedy for this awful condition? The precious blood of Jesus Christ. Through Christ we have been redeemed from the curse of the law. Not only are we liberated from the curse, but God has also established a new law within us—the law of the Spirit of life. Through Jesus the very life of God has been released on the inside of us. This means that death, poverty, and sickness no longer have the legal right to confine us anymore. *Life* is the Greek word *zoe*, which refers to the same life God has in Himself. Have you taken the time to consider the implications of the life of God dwelling inside of you? If the law of the Spirit of life is working within you, then this law will cancel and expel the law of sin and death. The power of the Spirit will put to death sickness and disease in your body. You no longer have to be bound by sickness because life is at work in you. If you are battling cancer, diabetes, autoimmune disorders, or any terminal illness, then be encouraged today because the same Spirit that was present in the beginning of creation resides within you. Declare out of your mouth: "The law of the Spirit of life in Christ has made me free from the law of sin and death; therefore, sickness must leave me now." You are not a victim. Your body is the temple of the Holy Spirit.

HEALING PRAYER

Father, in Jesus's name, I thank You that the very life of God dwells in me and brings Your manifest presence to every fiber of my being. I declare that sickness no longer has the right to dwell in me, because the law of the Spirit of life in Christ is at work in my mortal body. I command cancer, diabetes, lupus, Crohn's, MS, autoimmune disorders, fibromyalgia, gout, HIV/AIDS, and any other disease, symptom, or infirmity to die in Jesus's name. I am free from the bondage of sin and death, and I appropriate my freedom now. Thank You, Lord, for giving me eternal life. I recognize and proclaim that this eternal life is working in me here and now, not just when I get to heaven. I believe that through Jesus Christ the very life of God has been released inside of me, and I pray that You will reveal to me the ramifications of this amazing truth. I give You praise, in Jesus's name, amen!

Day 33

RISE!

HEALING MEDITATION

*Jesus saith unto him, Rise, take up
thy bed, and walk.* —John 5:8

We serve a compassionate and loving God. He longs to see us well, fulfilling the purpose and plan He has for our lives. This is the entire agenda of heaven when it comes to healing: God wants to restore us in spirit, soul, and body. In the Gospel of John, Jesus went to the pool of Bethesda and He encountered an impotent man. In the culture of the day, the inability to walk was equated with death, because you could not function, work, or provide for your family in such a condition. This man had been in an impotent state for 38 years. Can you imagine the severity of this situation? Jesus saw His condition and asked him a profound question, "Wilt thou be made whole?" (John 5:6). God is asking us the same question today. We must make up our minds what we want before we can truly embrace anything God has to offer us. To this question, the impotent man came up with several excuses. He asserted that he had been in the condition for a long period of time, and that there was no one to help him. Does this sound familiar? Like many people today, he couldn't see that the Living Word was all he needed to transform his life. You may be in an impotent condition in your life today. Don't allow the length of your struggle or the lack of support deter you from God's Word. Jesus ignored every one of the man's excuses and simply said, "Rise!" This word is filled with power. It means to awake from the sleep of death. God is saying the same to you and me today. Rise, take up your bed, and walk. No more excuses for your sickness. Today is the day of your freedom. Today is the day you will be made whole.

HEALING PRAYER

Father, in accordance with Your Word, I decree and declare that I am made whole by the power of the Holy Spirit. Every arthritic condition that plagues my body is reversed because of Your Word, Lord Jesus. I also speak to my kidneys, liver, central nervous system, heart, brain, muscle tissue, immune system, lungs, white blood cells, bones, joints, and bone marrow, and declare that they rise up in health and strength this very moment. Lord Jesus, I recognize Your Word is filled with the omnipotent power of God. Through Your Word I receive strength to walk in divine health and wholeness in my spirit, soul, and body. From this day forward I arise, take up my bed, and walk. I refuse to make any more excuses for why I am not experiencing the life You have ordained for me. Thank You for being the God who heals all of my diseases. In Jesus's name I pray all of these things. Amen.

RESURRECTION POWER

HEALING MEDITATION

But ye shall receive power, after that the
Holy Ghost is come upon you: and ye shall
be witnesses unto Me both in Jerusalem, and
in all Judaea, and in Samaria, and unto the
uttermost part of the earth. —Acts 1:8

One of my favorite subjects in school was science. My mother taught biology, chemistry, and earth science for nearly 25 years. As you can imagine, I was forced to do well in these disciplines. I was particularly fascinated with the study of force, power, and motion. Force is defined as strength or energy as an attribute of physical action or movement. In other words, force is what facilitates movement. In the book of Acts Jesus told His disciples to wait for the promise of the Father. What was the promise of the Father? It was nothing other than the baptism of the Holy Spirit. They were not to make a single move until they received this promise. Jesus said that when they received this promise, they would receive power—*dynamis*, which means explosive power or resident power (Strong's, G1411). In essence, it is resurrection power. Even though the disciples already had spiritual authority, they lacked spiritual power. We need both to see the manifestation of God's promises in our lives; we need both to deal with sickness and disease. It is like a police officer who has a badge yet possesses no gun. Essentially, he will be unable to stop criminals. Why? Even though he has the authority to arrest assailants, he does not have the power to bring them under subjection to his authority. The same is true of you and me. We can have knowledge of the Word of God, but without power we will not see movement. The Holy Spirit is the source of supernatural power. He is the One who breathes on the Word of God and makes it come alive inside of us. He is the One who enables us to drive sickness out of our lives and the lives of those we love. This power dwells in us by virtue of the Holy Spirit. Sickness is no match for the power of the Holy Spirit in you. Be encouraged today!

HEALING PRAYER

Father, in the name of Jesus, I thank You for Your resurrection power. Through You I am enabled to live the life You intended. I acknowledge the Holy Spirit as the source of this life-giving power at work in my inward man. Your Word declares that we shall receive power after the Holy Ghost has come upon us; so Lord, fill me with Your Spirit afresh. I command the mountain of sickness to be removed in Jesus's name. Every spirit of infirmity and disease must leave my body now. Thank You, Lord, that there is no sickness that can withstand the supernatural power of God. Right now, by faith, I release this supernatural power from the inside out, and I declare that this power is dynamic in its working. These things I ask in the precious name of Your Son Jesus Christ. Amen!

Day 35

FAITH IS THE KEY

HEALING MEDITATION

*And Jesus answering saith unto them, Have
faith in God. For verily I say unto you, That
whosoever shall say unto this mountain, Be thou
removed, and be thou cast into the sea; and shall
not doubt in his heart, but shall believe that those
things which he saith shall come to pass; he shall
have whatsoever he saith.* —Mark 11:22-23

One of the most important aspects of our ability to receive and walk in divine healing is faith. Faith is paramount to the Christian life. It is through faith that we are positioned to experience the benefits and blessings of God. Interestingly enough, faith is very simple but very misunderstood. I would dare to say that faith is one of the most misunderstood subjects in the church. In the book of Mark, Jesus told His disciples, "Have faith in God." Literally, He was telling them, "Have the faith *of* God." The word used for *faith* here is the word *pistis*, which includes the idea of confidence, and "conviction of the truth of anything," specifically God in this case (Strong's, G4102). Simply put, faith is confidence in God's Word. When we are walking in faith, we are convinced that God is exactly who He says He is and that He will do exactly what He says He will do. It is not enough to read the Bible; we must hear the revelation of the Holy Spirit from the words we read. Romans 10:17 says that faith comes by hearing and hearing comes by the Word—the *rhema*—of God. It is significant that the Bible uses the same word in Luke 4:4 and Romans 10:17. Real faith is not moved by what we see or feel; it is solely based on God's Word alone. It is more than just naming it and claiming it. It is not just about positively affirming the things we desire; it is the very Word of God itself. Walking in faith is about having a revelation by the Spirit of God that the Word of God is absolutely true, to the point that we will take action because of it. What are you faced with today? Through faith in the Word of God, you can quench all the fiery darts of the enemy. Faith is the key!

HEALING PRAYER

Father, in the name of Jesus, thank You for the gift of faith. Through faith in Your Word I can move every mountain of adversity in my life. I declare that whatever things I ask for in prayer, believing, I will receive. I believe Your Word; therefore, I receive my miracle now. Nothing can convince me that Your Word shall not surely come to pass in my life today. I stand upon the substance and substructure of Your Word, convinced that all You have promised has already been accomplished through the finished work of the cross of Christ. I take Your Word to heart—thank You for showing me how I should act on it. I place a demand today upon that finished work, fully expecting to see it manifested in every area of my life. In Jesus's name I ask these things. Amen.

Day 36

THE NAME OF JESUS

That at the name of Jesus every knee should bow,
of things in heaven, and things in earth, and
things under the earth. —Philippians 2:10

There was an old adage that I heard growing up: "What's in a name?" This phrase stood out to me because even as a child I was always fascinated with names. A person's name represents their identity and uniqueness. In Bible days, a name meant even more than that. In fact, your name is what determined your purpose and destiny. It comes from the Greek word *onoma*, and it signifies everything the thought or feeling aroused in the mind by mentioning, hearing, or remembering (Strong's, G3686). It represents a person's rank, authority, and power. Every name we hear invokes a feeling inside of us. The name of Jesus is the most powerful name in the universe. The Bible says that every knee will bow to that name, including everything in heaven, earth, and hell. There is no greater authority, rank, or power than in Jesus Christ. When is the last time you conceived of the name of Jesus in this way? Praying in Jesus's name is not a matter of religious jargon or properly ending a sentence. The name of Jesus invokes the power and authority of the kingdom of God. It causes sickness, disease, and infirmity to bow. Remember, it is not about your name; it's about His name. Every demon that exists must flee when we use the name of Jesus, and angels are dispatched through the name of Jesus. The presence of God is manifested with the name of Jesus. So no matter where you are or what you are facing, use the name of Jesus in the midst of your situation. Command every disease to leave in Jesus's name. His name is the highest authority in the land, which means it is impossible to be a victim when you know His name. Are there symptoms in your body? Call on the name of Jesus in faith and you will see the manifestation of His power in your life.

HEALING PRAYER

Father, I thank You for the name of Jesus. Your Word declares that the name of the Lord is a strong tower; the righteous run into it and are saved (see Proverbs 18:10). I declare that I am hidden behind the name of Jesus. I release Your authority over every situation I face in my life. There is nothing more powerful than Your name, Lord Jesus; therefore, I stand with bold confidence, knowing that I am protected in You. Every disease known to man must bow at the mention of Your name. I command cancer, lupus, diabetes, MS, Crohn's, arthritis, migraines, stroke, high blood pressure, skin diseases, reproductive issues, and any other disease, dysfunction, or infirmity to bow to the name of the Lord Jesus. Your Word declares that whosoever calls on the name of the Lord shall be delivered; therefore, I declare that I am delivered in Jesus's name. Amen!

Day 37

THE EVIDENCE OF UNSEEN THINGS

HEALING MEDITATION

*Through faith we understand that the
worlds were framed by the word of God, so
that things which are seen were not made of
things which do appear.* —Hebrews 11:3

Everything about our faith in God deals with our ability to stand firm even when there seems to be no results. Remember, the Word of God is what created the visible realm, though God Himself dwells behind the veil of invisibility. The Word of God tells us that if we have faith, our faith stands as proof that what we are believing God to do will surely manifest. Just because something is unseen does not mean it is unreal. For example, a woman who had cancerous growths on her back came to a ministry session with my wife and me. After speaking life over her body, we felt the tangible presence of God. There was no physical manifestation of healing that night; at least that is what we assumed. Two days later, however, we received a report that the growths on her back had fallen off. What happened? God happened! The moment we declared the Word of God in faith, the power of God began moving on her behalf. The growths were already dead the moment we prayed. Her miracle took place in the realm of the unseen first. If you are believing God for a miracle today, then be encouraged. It's already yours! Don't be confined by what you see. Keep declaring the promises of God by faith. Keep believing the Word of God is more powerful than the natural circumstances you may be facing. Your faith is the evidence of your miracle. Just like clouds are evidence of the coming rain, so your confidence in God serves as the catalyst for your healing. Remember, the attitude of expectation is the atmosphere for the miraculous. Don't allow the enemy to deceive you into thinking that just because you can't see it with your natural eyes, it doesn't exist. The moment you believed you received!

HEALING PRAYER

Father, in the name of Jesus, I thank You that Your Word is tried and true. The Word of God declares that the things seen were not made of things which do appear; therefore, I declare that I already possess my miracle. Healing is the divine right of every believer, and I refuse to allow the enemy of my soul to violate my kingdom rights. Right now, I have bold confidence in You, and this confidence acts as a catalyst for Your miraculous power in my life. I expect good things today! Just as the Word of God framed the world, I decree that my mindset and outlook are being established by the Word of God too. I am no longer confined to this natural realm, but I walk by faith and not by sight. I am already healed today. I am already delivered. I have already received my miracle in Jesus's name. Amen.

Day 38

HEALING VERSUS FEELING

HEALING MEDITATION

*Who His own self bare our sins in His own
body on the tree, that we, being dead to sins,
should live unto righteousness: by whose
stripes ye were healed.* —1 Peter 2:24

Oftentimes people struggle with the notion of being healed because they do not feel like they are healed. Quite frankly, healing is not a feeling. The word for *healed* in 1 Peter 2:24 is *iaomai*, which means "to cure" or "make whole" (Strong's, G2390). This healing is an act of God's grace manifested in Christ, which occurred in the past tense. First Peter 2:24 does not say He will heal us; it says we *were* healed. This is very important to understand. When Christ hung on the cross, dying for the sins of humanity more than two thousand years ago, He was reconciling the world to Himself. He was healing us. The Bible says, "To wit, that God was in Christ, reconciling the world unto Himself, not imputing their trespasses unto them; and hath committed unto us the word of reconciliation" (2 Corinthians 5:19). Our healing is a done deal. The price was already paid. The money has already changed hands. Whether or not you or I feel healed is completely irrelevant. Our healing is as much a reality as the sun rising every morning. Whether it feels hot or not has no bearing on the reality of the sun's existence. Even in the winter, when the temperature is at its coldest, the sun still rises every morning. The Bible does not say that "by His stripes ye feel healed." It says, "By His stripes ye were healed." So you need to pick yourself up, dust yourself off, and proclaim that you are the healed of the Lord Jesus regardless of your feelings and emotions. Take control of your feelings with the Word of God. Command your body and mind to come under the subjection of the Lord Jesus. All you have to do is believe the simple truth that you are healed! You are not going to be healed—you are healed. Every time we are faced with challenges in our bodies, we have to decide what the truth is: Is it what we feel or what God says?

HEALING PRAYER

Father, I declare that there is only one truth: Your Word. I acknowledge Your holy Word as the highest and final authority in my life. I declare that all of my feelings and emotions must bow to Your Word. I am not motivated by what I see, hear, or feel; I am only motivated by the Word of God. I recognize that Your Word is Your will for my life. I can rely on Your Word for anything that pertains to me. I am the healed of the Lord because Your Word declares I am. I recognize the deception involved with trusting my feelings and emotions, and I choose to only be governed by the supernatural reality of the Word of God at work on the inside of me. I know that the natural circumstances of my life are only temporary. Thank You, Lord, for transforming my thinking from being governed by my feelings to being governed by Your Word. Amen!

THE PERFECT LAW OF LIBERTY

HEALING MEDITATION

But whoso looketh into the perfect law of liberty, and continueth therein, he being not a forgetful hearer, but a doer of the work, this man shall be blessed in his deed. —James 1:25

When you think of a mirror, what comes to mind? A mirror brings clarity and perspective. The sole purpose of a mirror is to display things as they appear in reality. It doesn't matter how we think things look, a mirror usually reveals to us the truth. We make sure we are dressed properly and well furnished by looking in a mirror. In the book of James, the Word of God is likened to a mirror by which we ought to examine ourselves. Whatever the Word of God says is the truth. In fact, we become what we behold. The Bible refers to the Word of God as the perfect law of liberty. By law, we are not talking about legalism here, but we are talking about the irrevocable truth by which God governs His kingdom. The psalmist says, "The law of the Lord is perfect, converting the soul" (Psalm 19:7). In essence we are changed by the Word of God. It is filled with the miracle-working power of God. The simple truth is that the Word of God is the basis for all freedom and victory in our lives. You can rest assured that God's Word is perfect, even when you are not. As we gaze into this "perfect law of liberty," we are conformed into the image it reflects. In the natural you may be facing sickness and disease, but in the realm of the Spirit the perfect law of liberty says you are healed. Unlike a natural mirror, it is not enough to gaze in the Word periodically. The Bible declares that we must "continue therein." Just like a portable mirror you keep in your pocket, we have to remind ourselves 24 hours a day of who God says we are. Don't be a forgetful hearer, but be a doer of the Word. As you do what you see (from looking in the mirror of the Word), it will manifest the blessing of God in your life.

HEALING PRAYER

Father, I thank You for Your goodness and Your great love toward me. I declare I am free because the perfect law of liberty is at work within me, making me everything You intend for me to be. I make a conscious decision to gaze at Your Word only, and to not be moved by what I see in the natural realm. Whatever Your Word says is the truth. As I come to know the truth, the truth makes me free. I declare that my ears are attentive, my mind is alert, and my spirit is receptive to the Word of God. I will hear Your Word, receive Your Word, and be transformed by Your Word. No matter what the natural realm displays, I am totally convinced that the only mirror capable of displaying things as they really are is the Word of God. Thank You for lasting healing, deliverance, and freedom through Your all-powerful Word. I declare that I am completely healed from the crown of my head to the soles of my feet (spirit, soul, and body). In Jesus's name I pray, amen!

Day 40

LIFE AND DEATH

HEALING MEDITATION

I call heaven and earth to record this day against you, that I have set before you life and death, blessing and cursing: therefore choose life, that both thou and thy seed may live. —Deuteronomy 30:19

In the Old Testament, God revealed Himself to the children of Israel as their Great Deliverer. After 430 years of oppression, He brought them out with a mighty hand. They crossed the Red Sea on dry ground and saw their enemies, the Egyptians, utterly destroyed. As they went through the wilderness, God gave them His Word as the law that would govern everything they did from that point on. In the book of Deuteronomy, God told His people that they had a choice to make. What was this choice? They could either choose life or death. Did you know that the same choice is before you today? We have to make the choice for ourselves. Maybe you never thought about the challenges you are facing as a choice between life and death. So many people are suffering and hurting because they have chosen death instead of life. When I pray for the sick, the first thing I ask them is, "What do you want God to do for you?" This is a very important question. Healing is before you, but will you choose it? Will you decide to make the Word of God the final authority in your life? Will you choose to walk in the abundant life God has so graciously provided for you? You don't have to suffer unnecessarily. All you have to do is obey God's instructions. The Bible declares that if you choose life, you and your seed will live. I don't know about you, but this promise sounds good to me. The word *life* used in this passage means "to revive." God wants to revive you. He wants to heal and restore every area of your life; He's waiting on you to make the choice. You can be whole! You can live the abundant life! Just like the man at the pool of Bethesda, Jesus is asking you today, "Will you be made whole?" Choose life.

HEALING PRAYER

Father, in the name of Jesus, I come to You now as my Deliverer. You know my needs and the things affecting my life. Right now, I claim the promise of Your Word according to Romans 10:8-11, that whosoever calls on the name of the Lord shall be delivered. In the name of the Lord Jesus Christ, deliver me and set me free from any and all oppression of the enemy. I choose to live and not die. Thank You that Your supernatural life is working in me and reviving me. Sickness, disease, and oppression are not Your will for me. Your Word declares that You came for me to have life and have it more abundantly; therefore, I choose to live. I will never allow the enemy to rob me of the life God intends for me again. I choose to obey the Word of the Lord with my whole heart, and to meditate in its precepts day and night. Thank You for the blessing of wholeness. In Jesus's name I ask, amen.

Day 41

HEALING AND LOVE

*He that loveth his brother abideth in the
light, and there is none occasion of stumbling
in him. But he that hateth his brother is in
darkness, and walketh in darkness, and knoweth
not whither he goeth, because that darkness
hath blinded his eyes.* —1 John 2:10-11

The reality is that love is essential to the Christian life. As a matter of fact, the Bible tells us that without love we are nothing. We were made for love! So what does love have to do with healing? Everything! You must understand that the reason God heals anyone is because of His love for them. Therefore, healing is a manifestation of God's love for us. So many believers are suffering in their bodies because they are not walking in love toward their brothers and sisters in Christ. We have prayed for countless people who have been plagued with all types of chronic conditions and ailments, all because they refuse to forgive people who have hurt or wounded them. The nature of love is forgiveness, and when we forgive it empowers our love walk. As a result, we are able to experience God's miraculous power in our hearts and lives. The Bible says that "he that loveth his brother abideth in the light," and there is "none occasion of stumbling in him." *Stumbling* is the Greek word *skandalon*, and it means a "trap or snare" (Strong's, G4625). In other words, when you and I are not walking in love, we run the risk of falling into the snare of the enemy. The devil seeks to enslave us to sickness, poverty, and disease. What is the remedy for this? Love! Make sure you are walking in love at all costs. Examine your heart continually to see if there is anyone you have resentment toward or that you have yet to forgive. Refuse to abide in darkness. Do not allow Satan to have a foothold in your mind, body, or soul. The moment you release people for their offense, you are in a posture to receive your healing. Would you rather be angry or healed? The choice is yours today!

HEALING PRAYER

Father, in Jesus's name, I thank You for who You are and all that You have done. I thank You that two thousand years ago You sent Your Son Jesus Christ to die on the cross for my sins. You took upon Yourself all of my diseases so that I could walk in health and freedom. I recognize this as a manifestation of Your great love for me. As a result, I have a responsibility to walk in love toward my brothers and sisters. Right now, as an act of my free will, I forgive all who have offended, wounded, rejected, mistreated, or hurt me as I desire You to forgive me. I receive Your love for me now! As I release my offenders, I receive healing in my physical body. I declare that every symptom associated with not walking in love must leave me now, including arthritis, gout, chronic pain, high blood pressure, autoimmune disorders, and cancer. I command sickness and disease to leave my body in Jesus's name. Amen.

Day 42

THE POWER OF COMMUNION

For I have received of the Lord that which also I delivered unto you, that the Lord Jesus the same night in which He was betrayed took bread: and when He had given thanks, He brake it, and said, Take, eat: this is My body, which is broken for you: this do in remembrance of Me. After the same manner also He took the cup, when He had supped, saying, This cup is the new testament in My blood: this do ye, as oft as ye drink it, in remembrance of Me. —1 Corinthians 11:23-25

There are many born-again, Spirit-filled believers who are being tormented because they do not recognize the true significance of communion. Every time we take the communion of the body and blood of Jesus Christ, we are releasing divine healing. Why? Because He is our Passover Lamb. He took upon Himself our sicknesses and diseases. It does not matter what the sickness or disease may be, Christ overcame it on the cross. Every time we take communion, we testify of His victory and demonstrate His supernatural power over sickness. While my wife was pregnant with our third child, she was diagnosed with gestational diabetes. This was very irritating for us, seeing that we are people who minister divine healing to others. When we received the news, we began to pray. I declared to my wife that she was healed, and she agreed. I went on further to tell her that she would go to the doctor's office and hear a reversal of this evil report. Between the time we were given the news and the time she returned to the doctor, my wife and I and a few family members had devotions in the mornings. On a particular morning, we took communion and declared that my wife was healed. We thanked God for the victory. On her next doctor's visit, her blood test came back negative for diabetes. It is amazing how the simple act of partaking of the bread and wine (juice) in faith and expectation could have such a tremendous spiritual impact on us. It is a further picture of the healing plan of God in Christ.

HEALING PRAYER

Thank You, Jesus, for all You have done for me! Your precious body was broken for me, and Your blood was shed for me. Therefore, I take authority over any and all forms of sickness and disease, and I declare that they are not permitted to live here anymore! You are my Passover Lamb, who has caused the spirit of death, poverty, and sickness to pass over me forever. As I take of Your holy communion in faith, I believe that I receive complete and total healing from any and all sickness in my mind, body, and soul! I command every lying symptom operating illegally to cease and desist in Jesus's name. Thank You, Lord, for being my Healer. Amen!

Day 43

THE POWER OF THE RISEN CHRIST

But if the Spirit of Him that raised up Jesus from the dead dwell in you, He that raised up Christ from the dead shall also quicken your mortal bodies by His Spirit that dwelleth in you. —Romans 8:11

Have you ever thought about what it took to raise Jesus from the dead? We often read passages of Scripture in the Bible and simply move on rather than mull them over. What would it take to cause our Savior to awaken beyond the grave and conquer all of the powers of hell and death, and to rise victorious over the kingdom of darkness? Some would say, "Jesus was God!" Yes, this is true, but He went to the cross and died as a mortal man. The Bible says that it was the power of the Holy Spirit that quickened Jesus out of a state of death. Can you imagine Satan's surprise when He saw Jesus get up from the grave? He probably had a heart attack! What is even more amazing is the fact that the same Spirit that raised Christ from the dead dwells inside of you and me. The same all-powerful eternal Spirit at work in the Son of God is at work in you. Just as the Spirit quickened the Son of Man, so He quickens your mortal body. To quicken simply means to make alive. The Spirit of God on the inside of us produces life in our physical bodies. This means that sickness is no match for the resurrection power dwelling on the inside of you. If God's power can raise Jesus from the dead, then cancer doesn't stand a chance! You must change your way of thinking. You must realize who dwells in you and what He has made available for you. From now on, when a symptom touches your body, you need to open your mouth and declare, "The same Spirit that raised Jesus from the dead dwells in me and now quickens my mortal body; therefore, this symptom doesn't stand a chance!" The Spirit of God on the inside of you is regenerating you on a cellular level. Before anyone ever prays for you, the life of God within you is already destroying sickness and disease.

HEALING PRAYER

Father, I thank You that the same Spirit that raised Jesus from the dead dwells in me and now quickens my mortal body. There is life at work on the inside of me, and this life destroys the power of sickness and death. I decree that the power of all sickness is neutralized by the power of the Holy Spirit within me. As I release my faith, I receive healing and wholeness in my physical body. From this day forward I declare that I can no longer be a victim. There are no more excuses! Thank You, Lord, for Your eternal life, which effectually works in me here and now. In Jesus's name I pray, amen!

SATAN IS A LIAR

HEALING MEDITATION

Ye are of your father the devil, and the lusts of your father ye will do. He was a murderer from the beginning, and abode not in the truth, because there is no truth in him. When he speaketh a lie, he speaketh of his own: for he is a liar, and the father of it. —John 8:44

The devil is referred to in the Bible as the father of lies. This ought to help you understand how to respond to what the devil says. How would you respond to a compulsive liar? Soon you would begin to ignore what they say because you know they are not a credible source of information. If you know the devil is a liar, then why are you still listening to him? Every word that comes out of his mouth is a lie. He is a rascal and a vagabond bent on bringing you into captivity to his deception. How does he lie? By attempting to convince you that the Word of God is not true. This was his strategy in the Garden of Eden. The enemy beguiled Eve by contradicting the truth of God's Word. That "old serpent" does the same thing today. It can be in the form of a "lying symptom" in your body, and immediately the thought comes to your mind, "I must be sick"; or it can come in the form of an "evil report" or diagnosis from the doctor. There is one purpose to all of the examples I just mentioned—to get you to doubt God's Word and thereby cut you off from His blessing. This is especially true when it comes to healing. The devil does not want you to walk in divine health, so he will tell as many lies as possible to keep you sick. These lies come in the form of words, thoughts, and suggestions. Such lies include, "You have cancer," "You will not get well," "It runs in your family," or "God is teaching you a lesson with this sickness." How do you confront the lies of the enemy? You confront the devil's lies with the truth of God's Word. When he says that you can't, tell him that you can do all things through Christ who strengthens you. If he tells you that you will die, declare, "I will not die but live and declare the works of the Lord." It's time for you to put that liar in his place!

HEALING PRAYER

Father, in the name of Jesus, I thank You for exposing the lies of the evil one in my life. Through Your Word I am empowered by the truth, and Your truth overcomes every lie. I bring every word, thought, and suggestion into subjection to Your Word. Anything that contradicts Your Word is a lie, and I choose to reject it. Your Word declares I will know the truth and the truth will make me free. According to Your truth I am already healed, delivered, and set free. Greater is He that lives in me than he that is in the world. Thank You, Lord, for liberating me from any and all deception in whatever forms it may take. I praise You that I experience lasting freedom through Your truth. In Jesus's name I pray, amen.

HEALING BELONGS TO YOU!

HEALING MEDITATION

And the people, when they knew it, followed Him: and He received them, and spake unto them of the kingdom of God, and healed them that had need of healing. —Luke 9:11

Why did Jesus go about healing and setting people free from bondage? The Bible said the people knew Jesus and His apostles traveled to Bethsaida, so they followed them. Why did they follow them? It was because they realized Jesus had the power to heal them of whatever infirmity they possessed. Notice that Jesus did not turn them away. He did not say, "You don't deserve to be healed," or "Sickness is God's will for your life!" Instead, He gladly received them, communicated to them concerning the kingdom of God, and healed them. It was as if the people believed they were entitled to healing. What would happen if the body of Christ took on the same attitude of the people in the time of Jesus? What would be the outcome if we adopted the mindset that healing belongs to us? I can tell you what would happen—you would receive your healing! In fact, the word *need* in this passage is the Greek word *chreia*. At its root, this word means "necessity" or "to take for one's use" (Strong's, G5532). Simply put, healing belongs to you because of your covenant with God, and it is time for you to make use of it. You no longer have to wait passively for something to change in your physical circumstances, but you can lay hold on the covenant promise of healing right now. How desperate are you to take what is rightfully yours? It is no coincidence that the Bible says that they "followed Him." This is not a passive or distant pursuit, but it is from the word *akoloutheō*, and it means to join yourself to the company of another person or to side with their party (Strong's, G190). God wants us to side with Him as it relates to divine healing, and He says it belongs to you. Will you take your healing today?

HEALING PRAYER

Father, I thank You that You have given me the promise of healing as an act of Your love and compassion for me because of Your Son Jesus. Through the cross of Christ, the curse of sickness has been destroyed and I have been given the right to the Tree of Life. Thank You for the gift of divine healing and divine health. From this day forward I approach healing as something that belongs to me. You are a covenant God, and Your covenant with me says that You are my Great Physician. I cleave to this promise with bold faith and expectation, knowing that I will receive health and wholeness in every area of my life. Thank You for the covenant and healing. I declare that Your power is working effectually in me, enabling me to overcome every sickness, disease, ailment, and infirmity. I am more than a conqueror through Your great love for me. In the precious name of Jesus I pray, amen.

Day 46

STANDING ON
THE PROMISES

HEALING MEDITATION

Cast not away therefore your confidence, which hath great recompence of reward. For ye have need of patience, that, after ye have done the will of God, ye might receive the promise. —Hebrews 10:35-36

The Bible tells us in the book of Hebrews that we are not to cast away our confidence. When you ponder this statement, it immediately reveals that we have a part to play when it comes to cooperating with God for our healing. What does it mean to "cast away your confidence"?

In the Greek, to cast away (*apoballō*) means to throw off (Strong's, G577). The phrase "cast not away your confidence" means that you're not to throw away your free and fearless courage, bold assurance, and freedom in speech. This is a strong statement indeed. The enemy wants you to quit. He wants you to "throw in the towel." Why? Because every promise in the Word of God requires us to speak boldly and confidently in faith to receive it. Simply put, the devil wants us to stop talking. Our tendency is to become silent when things become difficult. We can retreat into a contemplative mode. This is not what God wants us to do. He wants us to lay hold of the promise of healing with bold confidence and assurance. This requires us to speak the promises of God over and over again. We have to declare with our mouths that God's Word cannot lie. We have to speak healing even when we don't feel like it. In doing so, we are standing on the promises of God. What is the benefit of not quitting? The Bible says there is a "great recompence of reward." This phrase means "payment of wages due." God promises to reward your endurance if you refuse to quit. One of the most important things to possess when it comes to believing God for your healing is patience (i.e., endurance). It is the will of God for you to endure in whatever situation you may find yourself in today. God wants you to keep speaking the Word no matter what! In doing so, you will eventually inherit the promise. Stand on the promises of God, beloved!

HEALING PRAYER

Father, in the name of Jesus, I thank You for the wonderful promises in Your Word. According to Isaiah 53:5 and 1 Peter 2:24, I am healed by the stripes of Jesus. I believe this promise with my whole heart, because You cannot lie; therefore, Your Word cannot lie. I boldly confess this promise out of my mouth and believe it in my heart: I am the healed of the Lord from the crown of my head to the soles of my feet. From this day forward I refuse to yield to the spirit of fear in any form it may manifest. I have confidence in Your Word, Lord! Thank You that through Your Word I am empowered to overcome every sickness and disease that exists. Nothing shall separate me from Your love. I am fully persuaded that I am already healed, and I stand on the promise of healing, knowing that it will manifest shortly. Thank You, Lord! In Jesus's name I pray. Amen!

Day 47

SALVATION TO THE SICK

HEALING MEDITATION

Is any sick among you? let him call for the elders of the church; and let them pray over him, anointing him with oil in the name of the Lord: and the prayer of faith shall save the sick, and the Lord shall raise him up; and if he have committed sins, they shall be forgiven him. —James 5:14-15

I want to let you in on a profound secret that has transformed my life and the lives of every person I have ministered to. The secret is this: sickness is evil. The devil has attempted to convince people that sickness is somewhat good. The reality is that there is no such thing as partial good or partial evil; there is only good or evil. Whatever you are facing in your body is either from God or the devil. (We also believe you have a responsibility to take care of your body.) If God is a good God, then why would He put something evil on you? The answer to this question is simple: He wouldn't and He doesn't. In the epistle of James, he tells the church that if there are any sick among them, they should call the elders for prayer. The elders are to anoint the sick with oil and pray the prayer of faith, and the sick will be saved. Notice the Bible didn't say that the sick would be healed. Rather, it says the sick will be saved. The word *saved* in this passage is the Greek word *sozo*, and it means to deliver from danger, peril, or evil (Strong's, G4982). This is an all-encompassing word, which implies that there is something the sick need to be delivered from. Why? Because healing is an act of God's grace. Just like sin, sickness is an evil from which people need deliverance. God does not want you sick. He wants you well! The sick experience salvation through the prayer of faith. The Bible tells us that the prayer of faith will save the sick. Just like we are saved through a sincere confession of faith in Christ, we are healed through our sincere confession of Christ as Lord. We don't have to toil or struggle with evil any longer. Whoever calls on the name of the Lord shall be saved. Call on the Healer in faith today and you will be delivered.

HEALING PRAYER

Father, in the name of Jesus Christ, I thank You for Your grace. Because I place my confidence in Your Word, I receive healing just as I received salvation. Jesus came to deliver me from the evils of sickness just as surely as He came to forgive my sin. Thank You for manifesting Your grace in every area of my life. I recognize that You have given me the promise of healing as an act of Your great love and compassion for me. I no longer have to tolerate sickness as something You allow to teach me a lesson or to prove Your sovereignty, but I now recognize sickness as evil. This very moment I receive my healing in the name of Jesus Christ. Amen!

Day 48

THEY SHALL RECOVER

HEALING MEDITATION

And these signs shall follow them that believe;
in My name shall they cast out devils; they
shall speak with new tongues; they shall take up
serpents; and if they drink any deadly thing, it
shall not hurt them; they shall lay hands on the
sick, and they shall recover. —Mark 16:17-18

The first thing you must accept if you want to experience healing and live a successful life in Christ is that the Word of God is the final authority over everything. Once God says it, you ought to believe it, and that should settle it. Oftentimes we are faced with things and people who attempt to contradict the Word of God. Religion and tradition have taught us to remain passive where God tells us to be aggressive. Well-meaning religious people may say things to you such as, "God might heal you if it is His will!" But the question is: If the Bible is our final authority, then how should we approach situations and circumstances? It is really quite simple. We should come under subjection to the Word of God. Whatever the Word of God says is what we should accept as absolute truth. The Bible says in Mark 16:18 that we shall lay hands on the sick and *they shall recover*. This is what you would call an absolute statement. In other words, when Jesus said it, He meant what He said. The word *shall* implies a promise. There are so many people who are unable to receive their healing or minister healing to others because they refuse to agree with God. Do you agree with God? Do you believe His Word is the final authority? If you believe, then you need to act on the Word. If you are dealing with the symptoms of sickness, lay hands on yourself. There may be a loved one or friend who needs to be healed. Lay hands on that friend and pray the prayer of faith, believing that God must honor His Word. Stop making excuses! The Bible never said that "the sick shall recover unless it is the will of God for them to be sick," nor did it say, "They shall recover from some sicknesses and not others." The bottom line is that the sick shall recover. All you have to do is believe the Word of God.

HEALING PRAYER

Father, in the name of Jesus Christ, I thank You that Your Word is the final authority in my life. Your Word declares that in Your name I will cast out devils, I will speak with new tongues, I will take up serpents, and I will lay hands on the sick and they shall recover. This includes me! Right now, in Jesus's name, I release Your power into my life and the lives of those around me. I declare that no sickness can dwell in my mortal body. I declare that I have the authority of Jesus on the inside of me, and through His shed blood I was healed of all manner of sickness, disease, and infirmity. Your Word says that I am healed; therefore, I am the healed of the Lord in Jesus's name. Amen.

Day 49

THE VALLEY OF DECISION

Multitudes, multitudes in the valley of decision: for the day of the Lord is near in the valley of decision. —Joel 3:14

There are so many people today who are uncertain as to whether or not they can receive their healing and walk in divine health. I have ministered to countless souls who are hurting and in despair. Many of them are wondering if God loves them and, if so, if there is a way out of their current struggle. You may be in that place this very moment. This is what the Bible calls the "valley of decision." In Scripture, valleys served two primary purposes: to grow corn and fight battles. It was ideal for fighting battles because of the low ground clearance and width. This was the place where you either conquered your enemy or became conquered. This conquest takes place in the mind of every believer. We must make a quality decision to conquer sickness. The Bible says in Joel 3:14 that multitudes are in the valley of decision. This is a prophetic passage referring to the Messiah and His second coming; however, I believe it represents the state of many in the body of Christ today. We all must make a choice. Are you going to walk in the fullness of God's promises for your life or are you going to bow to the hand of the enemy? The choice is yours. This is what the Word of God promises: "The day of the Lord is near in the valley of decision." This is not the time to stop trusting God; it is the time to believe Him more than ever before. The delivering hand of God is nearer than when you first believed. God has already vindicated you of your affliction; it is time for you to grab hold of the victory. The Word of God declares in Joel 3:16, "The Lord also shall roar out of Zion, and utter His voice from Jerusalem; and the heavens and the earth shall shake: but the Lord will be the hope of His people, and the strength of the children of Israel." He is your hope and your strength, and He will surely deliver you. Be encouraged today! God loves you and He is near.

HEALING PRAYER

Father, in the name of Jesus, I thank You that You never leave me or forsake me. Your Word declares that even though I walk through the valley of the shadow of death, You are with me. Today I make a quality decision to trust Your Word above any and everything else in my life. Lord Jesus, You conquered sickness and disease two thousand years ago; therefore, I choose to walk in victory over all sickness that comes against my life. I rest in Your finished work and I rejoice that I have the victory. Thank You, Father, that You have manifested Your great love and power in my life. Today is the day of my deliverance; today is the day of my salvation. Thank You, Lord, for delivering me from the hand of the enemy. In Jesus's name I ask this, amen.

Day 50

YOU SHALL BE MADE WHOLE

HEALING MEDITATION

But when Jesus heard it, He answered
him, saying, Fear not: believe only, and
she shall be made whole. —Luke 8:50

I love the Gospels. In them we see the marvelous love of Jesus being displayed toward His people. We are His people and He longs to see us healed and made whole. In the book of Luke, Jesus encounters a man by the name of Jairus whose daughter is deathly ill. This is his only daughter and she is only 12 years old. Can you imagine the desperation and pain that this father endured? While Jairus was making his appeal to our Lord, he received the news that his daughter was dead. What would you have done in this situation? Most people would have either blamed God for this tragedy or accepted it as His will. Instead of a story of tragedy, this becomes a story of restoration. Jesus, through a radical act of grace and compassion, intervenes and manifests His healing power. Jesus said to Jairus, "Fear not: believe only, and she shall be made whole." Why does Jesus tell him to "fear not"? God knows the torment fear produces. He knows the mindset of fear will undermine the very miracle we need. Instead of fearing, we are commanded to believe. The first thing we must believe is that it is the perfect will of God for us to be whole. Do you believe this? Believing is a deliberate act of faith and trust. You can't believe on accident. God specializes in turning impossible situations around for His glory and for your benefit. Like Jairus, God is telling you today, "Fear not. Wholeness belongs to you." That is a divine promise and God cannot break His promises. As you may have realized, that 12-year-old girl was resurrected from the dead. If God can resurrect someone from the dead to bring wholeness into their lives, how much more will He heal and deliver you who are still alive? Today is your day! You shall be made whole.

HEALING PRAYER

Father, I thank You for Your healing promises in my life. Just as You promised Jairus that his daughter would be made whole, I receive the promise of wholeness in my life. Thank You, Jesus, for setting me free from all bondage and healing me of all my diseases. According to my faith, I declare that I refuse to be in fear. I refuse to doubt Your Word. I decree that I am a person of bold faith and confidence in You. I am a believer and not a doubter. Doubt is no longer a part of my thought process or vocabulary. I rejoice because I know You are a good God, and Your Word shall surely come to pass in my life. Thank You in advance for my healing and wholeness in every area of my life. In Jesus's name I pray. Amen!

Day 51

OPEN YOUR EYES!

HEALING MEDITATION

And it came to pass, as He sat at meat with them, He took bread, and blessed it, and brake, and gave to them. And their eyes were opened, and they knew Him; and He vanished out of their sight. —Luke 24:30-31

In the world system, there exists a philosophy that says, "Seeing is believing!" Actually, this is completely false when it comes to the kingdom of God. We don't believe things because we can see them; we see things because we believe them. During the earthly ministry of Jesus, He taught His disciples the precepts of God's kingdom. Most of the time they did not have a clue as to what He was teaching. How could they have followed Him so passionately if they didn't know who He was nor understand His kingdom? It's quite simple, actually. Religion promotes the following of rules, people, and philosophies we do not understand. The disciples were simply being religious, but Jesus was calling them to a life of real faith. What was the turning point for the disciples? In the Gospel of Luke, Jesus broke bread with His disciples after His resurrection, and as soon as they partook of the bread, their eyes were opened. This expression comes from the Greek word *dianoigō*, and it means "to open thoroughly that which was once closed" (Strong's, G1272). What was closed? Their understanding. This was the turning point in the disciples' lives. For the first time they saw Jesus for who He really was. The moment you and I receive a revelatory understanding of who Jesus really is, we, like the disciples, will never be the same again. When you open your eyes to the truth that He is the Healer and that He always wants you well, you will believe on a whole new level. Remember, you are changed into what you see. God wants to open the eyes of your understanding today. He wants your faith to be ignited so that you will walk in a new dimension of His miraculous power.

HEALING PRAYER

Father, I thank You that Your Word brings revelation and truth to me now. I declare that the eyes of my understanding are open, and I know what is the hope of my calling, and the riches of my inheritance in You. Today I choose to see Your goodness and love toward me. I recognize You are my Deliverer, Healer, and Lord. I know deep down in my heart that every good gift comes from You and everything that is evil comes from the evil one. As I gaze into Your heart through the eyes of faith, I am transformed into Your image and likeness. Healing is mine. Deliverance is mine. Restoration is mine. I receive them now in the name of Jesus. Amen.

Day 52

YOU SHALL LIVE

HEALING MEDITATION

*I shall not die, but live, and declare the
works of the Lord.* —Psalm 118:17

I cannot speak for anyone else, but I can remember times where I honestly thought I was not going to make it. I had accepted a lie from the enemy. Does this sound familiar? It may come in the form of a doctor's report, a symptom of illness, or a spiritual attack from the forces of darkness. No matter what it is or how it looks, you must make a conscious decision to declare the Word of God over your situation. David, the psalmist and king of Israel, understood this truth. He declared in Psalm 118:12,

"They compassed me about like bees; they are quenched as the fire of thorns: for in the name of the Lord I will destroy them." The enemy was afflicting him; he was surrounded on every side. Like bees swarm around a person when they come near their honeycomb, so the enemy surrounded David. This is a tactic of intimidation and control. Why? It's because the enemy does not want you to obtain the blessing God has prepared for you. He does not want you to experience healing and breakthrough. Like David, you are going to have to open your mouth and declare, "I will live and not die!" It doesn't matter what the doctors say, you have a job to do and a purpose to fulfill. Don't give up now! You are too close to the "honeycomb." The devil may "sting" you, but he can't kill you because you have a covenant with Almighty God. Jesus came that you might have life and have it more abundantly. We recently received a testimony of a young lady who was diagnosed with stage three cancer. She got a hold of our teachings and began to declare that she was not going to die. She determined that cancer was not going to have the last word. Every day she spoke the promises of God over her life. After a very intense spiritual and physical battle, her physician declared that there was no cancer in her body. You shall live and not die!

HEALING PRAYER

Father, in the name of Jesus, I declare that I shall live and not die. I will declare the works of the Lord all the days of my life. Your Word says that with long life You will satisfy me. Thank You, Lord, for health and wholeness all the days of my life. From this day forward I refuse to be intimidated by the enemy. I refuse to accept any of his lies any longer. Lord Jesus, I come to You as my Deliverer, for You know everything that concerns me. You are aware of every frailty in my life, yet You choose to love me unconditionally. Right now, I receive Your zoe life in my mortal flesh. Never again will I yield to the evil report of the enemy, but I will set my eyes and hope on You. In Your name I will overcome every sickness, disease, infirmity, or hindrance. Amen!

Day 53

YOU ARE FORGIVEN

I write unto you, little children, because your sins are forgiven you for His name's sake. —1 John 2:12

D o you realize that you have been forgiven? This may seem like an obvious statement, but it contains supernatural implications you may not have considered before. What does it mean to be forgiven? The word *forgiveness* means to send away, to omit, or to let go. Simply put, to forgive is to release. Through the cross of Christ, God has released us from our sin. The shed blood of Jesus served as the payment for the penalty of our sin. Through this act of grace, you and I have been completely forgiven in

Christ. To illustrate the significance of forgiveness as it relates to healing, we can look at the Gospel of Matthew, where Jesus encounters a man with the palsy. As you know, palsy was a severe paralytic condition that prevented a person from performing most functions in their life. A person afflicted with this dreadful infirmity would most often be confined to a bed, unable to move without assistance. Jesus declared to the man with the palsy, "Thy sins are forgiven." To this, the religious spectators became hostile and resistant. Jesus said, "For whether is easier, to say, Thy sins be forgiven thee; or to say, Arise, and walk?" (Matthew 9:5). The implication is that forgiveness is a much greater miracle than healing. In the time of Christ, people attributed most sicknesses to sin. If God has forgiven us of all sins in Christ, then why would He allow us to remain in our sickness? The answer is that He doesn't! The real issue is this: Do you believe that you have been forgiven? If you do, then you must realize that the same God who washed away all of your sins is the same God who healed all of your diseases. Like the man with the palsy, you no longer have to be confined to a bed of guilt, shame, and condemnation, but you are free to "arise, take up your bed, and walk!" Don't you dare tolerate guilt and shame any longer, and don't you dare tolerate sickness and disease. They were both nailed to the cross, never to be imputed to you again. My friend, you are forgiven!

HEALING PRAYER

Father, in the name of Jesus Christ, I thank You that I have been forgiven of all of my sins—the ones that I know and the ones I don't know. Because of Your mercy toward me, I have been released from the bondage of guilt, shame, and condemnation. Through Your sovereign act of forgiveness, demonstrated by the cross, I have been eternally separated from the tentacles of sin, sickness, and death. I boldly declare that I am clean through Your Word and fully eligible to walk in divine health. As an act of faith and obedience, I now freely forgive all others as I would have You to forgive me. Thank You for forgiving me now and cleansing me with Your blood. I receive my healing with my whole heart today, in Jesus's mighty name, amen.

Day 54

HEALING IN THE ATONEMENT

HEALING MEDITATION

And not only so, but we also joy in God through our Lord Jesus Christ, by whom we have now received the atonement. —Romans 5:11

The atonement is central to an understanding of divine healing. Why? Because it represents the heart of God in restoring and redeeming His people. In the Old Testament, God gave the Israelites *Yom Kippur* (the Day of Atonement) as a temporary means to be exonerated from their sins. The sins of the whole nation were placed upon the scapegoat, who in turn was led away into the wilderness, never to be seen again. This represented the putting away of sin. The spotless lamb was sacrificed, symbolically washing Israel from their sin, which was a type and a shadow. In the New Covenant, Christ stood in the place of believers and received the wrath of God on their behalf. As a result, God can pour out His favor, goodness, and blessing on believers as they stand in the place of Christ. He stood in our place so that we can stand in His. He became a curse so that we could be made righteous. He was punished so that we could be rewarded. God's relationship with us is based on this positional reality: We have been placed in Christ, which is the most favorable position there is. What does this have to do with healing? Simple! This exchange between sin and holiness, unrighteousness and righteousness, also causes us to be able to receive perfect health in our physical bodies as a result of the curse being broken. The word for *atonement* in the New Testament means "to restore to favor through monetary exchange." Jesus purchased our healing on the cross. It was paid for in full! There is no question whether or not God wants you healed because He paid the highest price for your healing. This ought to make you a little more aggressive when the devil attempts to put sickness on your life, because he is causing you to suffer unnecessarily. The next time the enemy tries to attack your body, declare the blood of Jesus as the proof of purchase for your healing.

HEALING PRAYER

Father, in the name of Jesus, I thank You for who You are and all that You have done. Thank You for taking my place on the cross. Through You my sins have been forgiven and I have become a recipient of the atonement. Thank You, Lord, for taking my sin so that I could receive Your righteousness. Father, I accept the atonement for my sins as Your free gift of grace through Jesus Christ. Right now, I declare that because I have been made righteous in Christ, sickness no longer has the legal right to live in my body. Therefore, I command all ailments, illnesses, infirmities, and disorders to evacuate now. I will not accept anything that was not planted by the Lord Jesus Himself, and I declare my complete restoration in Your name. Amen!

ENOUGH IS ENOUGH

HEALING MEDITATION

And this did she many days. But Paul, being grieved, turned and said to the spirit, I command thee in the name of Jesus Christ to come out of her. And he came out the same hour. —Acts 16:18

Have you ever encountered a bully in your life? I have encountered several. Usually a bully will take your lunch money, embarrass you in front of your peers, or physically assault you—if you allow him. There comes a time, however, when you have to take a stand. In that moment when you are tired of all the jesting and the assaulting and the embarrassment, you have to let the bully know you are serious. The devil is a bully, and like all bullies, he thrives off of fear, intimidation, manipulation, and control. He knows he has but a short time to act out, so he does everything in his power to frustrate you. How do you deal with this? Paul encountered this spiritual bullying in Acts 16. There was a woman filled with the spirit of divination, which taunted Paul and his colleagues on their missionary journey. Finally, Paul became wearied by this satanic annoyance and declared, "I command thee in the name of Jesus to come out of her." In other words, he came to the place where enough was enough. If you want to walk in what God intends for your life, you must come to that same place of severity. You have to tell the enemy, "Enough is enough!" Tell the devil that you are tired of him stealing your health, you are tired of him oppressing your mind, and you will no longer tolerate him stealing your joy. Like all bullies, when you give him enough resistance, he will stand down. Deep down Satan is a coward and a sore loser. Put him in his place! Declare, "Sickness can't stay any longer!" If you want to walk in your healing, you have to come to a place where you actually hate sickness with all your heart. The notion of you or a loved one being sick should anger you. You have had enough oppression from the devil. It is time to hasten the victory and declare, "Enough is enough!"

HEALING PRAYER

Father, I come to You in the name of Your Son Jesus Christ, the name by which every knee must bow, of things in heaven, on this earth, and under the earth. I declare in the matchless name of Jesus that anything in my life—sickness, disease, depression, anger, or spiritual oppression—must cease right now. Your Word says that You have given me authority to tread on serpents, scorpions, and over all the power of the enemy, and nothing shall by any means hurt me; therefore, I no longer tolerate Satan's bullying and manipulation in my life and in the lives of those around me. I trample down all of the enemy's operations in my life and in the lives of those around me in the name of Jesus. Amen.

Day 56

SICKNESS IS EVIL

HEALING MEDITATION

How God anointed Jesus of Nazareth with the Holy Ghost and with power: who went about doing good, and healing all that were oppressed of the devil; for God was with Him. —Acts 10:38

Several year ago I experienced a spiritual epoch concerning healing. Even though I had believed in divine healing and walked in it for quite some time, I still had a tolerance for sickness. You must understand religion teaches us to tolerate the devil's schemes under the guise that "God allows it." I subconsciously believed this religious lie, until one day the Lord revealed to me through the Word of God that sickness was never His will. The Bible tells us in Acts 10 that Jesus was anointed by God through the Holy Spirit to go about healing and releasing God's people from the oppression of Satan. Notice that the Bible equates sickness with the oppression of the devil. Simply put, sickness is evil! Imagine someone you are friends with told you that they were hosting a murderer on the run in their home until they became "established." What would you say to them? You would probably warn them of the serious repercussions of aiding and abetting a criminal. By allowing a criminal to live in your home, you would be a putting everyone around you in grave danger, not to mention the fact that you would be breaking the law. Well, this is exactly what many Christians are doing. They are unwittingly aiding and abetting Satan through their passivity toward sickness. When you recognize that sickness is an evil work that Jesus Himself came to destroy, you will be less likely to tolerate it in your life or the lives of the people you care about. Allow the Lord to renew your mind through the Word of God. The basic definition of holiness is to love what God loves and to hate what God hates. God hates sickness and so should you. On the other hand, God loves it when His children are walking in divine health and healing.

HEALING PRAYER

Father, I thank You that it is Your will that I walk in perfect health. Lord, I acknowledge that sickness is not Your will for my life but is from the enemy. I rebuke every satanic oppression in my body that is designed to keep me from fulfilling my God-given destiny. And I thank You, Lord, that I am anointed, just as Jesus was anointed when He was on the earth, with the Holy Ghost and with power, to do good and to heal all who are oppressed by the enemy. I fall out of agreement with the enemy in all areas of my life. I will no longer accept the lies of Satan. I am the healed of the Lord in Jesus's name, amen!

Day 57

ENCOURAGE YOURSELF

HEALING MEDITATION

And David was greatly distressed; for the people
spake of stoning him, because the soul of all the
people was grieved, every man for his sons and
for his daughters: but David encouraged himself
in the Lord his God. —1 Samuel 30:6

The famous Dr. Martin Luther King Jr. once said, "The ultimate measure of a man is not where he stands in moments of comfort and convenience, but where he stands at times of challenge and controversy." There is something about trials and difficulties that reveal our faith and character. There are many people who say they trust God and believe He is their Healer, but when they experience opposition to that profession, they become offended with Him. David did not respond in this way. When the enemy infringed on his camp and took his family, he was faced with tremendous distress and grief. The people spoke of stoning him. At this point, David had a choice to make— he could give in to his emotions or he could choose to trust God in spite of the trial. Interestingly enough, the Bible says that David "encouraged himself in the Lord." What does it mean to encourage yourself in the Lord? *Encourage*, in the Hebrew, means to "strengthen yourself." How do we strengthen ourselves in the Lord? We strengthen ourselves by reminding ourselves of God's promises. Instead of becoming discouraged by the evil report of the devil, we remind ourselves of who God says we are and what God says belongs to us. Refuse to bow down to sickness or disease. Don't become frustrated at God over the circumstances. This is a trick of the enemy to disempower you and cause you to become a victim. You are a victor! Greater is He that lives in you than he that is in the world. You are more than a conqueror in Christ, and this trial, struggle, or sickness is not unto death, but God will be glorified. The Bible tells us in Ephesians 5:19 that we are to "speak to ourselves." You need to give yourself a spiritual pep talk every now and then. This is exactly what David did and, in the end, he recovered all. Speak the Word over yourself and you will experience a complete and total recovery. Be encouraged today!

HEALING PRAYER

Father, I thank You for who You are and all that You have done. Right now, in the name of Jesus, I speak over myself and declare, even as Jesus declared, "It is finished." Therefore, I am not moved by what I feel and I am not moved by what I see; I am not moved by what I hear or even the doctor's report; I am only moved by the Word of God. Your Word is truth and is my reality. In the name of Jesus, I thank You that Your Word says that I shall not die, but live and declare the works of the Lord. I am an overcomer because greater is He that is in me than he that is in the world. I encourage myself in the Lord today, in Jesus's name. Amen!

LESSONS FROM A LEPER

HEALING MEDITATION

And one of them, when he saw that he
was healed, turned back, and with a loud
voice glorified God. —Luke 17:15

L eprosy was the most debilitating disease during the time of Christ. There was almost nothing worse than leprosy, besides physical death itself. As a matter of fact, most lepers were as good as dead. They were not allowed to function in normal society due to their condition and they were often forced to live outside of the city and beg for money. In Luke's Gospel Jesus encountered ten lepers. Without even touching them, He commanded them to go and show themselves to the priest. As they went, they were cleansed from their leprosy. However, only one of the lepers turned back to give glory to God. Jesus responded to this act of faith by saying, "Arise, go thy way: thy faith hath made thee whole" (Luke 17:19). We can learn some valuable lessons from this leper. The first thing we can learn is that there is no condition God is not willing and able to heal. There was nothing worse than leprosy, yet Jesus healed them. What a loving God we serve. The second lesson is the truth that God desires wholeness for you. It wasn't a complete miracle until they were completely restored. The word *whole* in this passage is the Greek word *sozo*, which means to heal, deliver, and to keep (Strong's, G4982). What was the key? The leper's faith. All he had to do was believe that Jesus was who He said He was and that He had done what He said He would do. Acknowledgement is powerful! Begin to thank God that you are already healed. Worship Him right now! Don't wait to see the manifestation of your healing—do it now! As you worship Him in faith, you will experience wholeness.

HEALING PRAYER

Father, I thank You for the love You have for me and that it is Your will I am healed, restored, and made whole in every area of my life. I praise You for what You have done and I thank You for restoring me. I thank You, Lord, that You began a good work in me and You will complete it until the day of Christ. I have absolute faith and confidence in Your Word and I know You are Jehovah Rapha, my Great Physician. I will not wait for my circumstances to change before I praise You; but I praise You now, with all of my heart, in faith, and I rejoice in hope. And I know that it is already done. In Jesus's name I pray. Amen.

HE HEALED THEM ALL

HEALING MEDITATION

*But when Jesus knew it, He withdrew Himself
from thence: and great multitudes followed Him,
and He healed them all.* —Matthew 12:15

One of the most disturbing and widely held beliefs I find in the church is the notion that healing is not for everyone. I have heard ministers teach this false doctrine from the pulpit several times. In other words, they claim that God may heal some people but not others. Beloved, this is not biblical. If this were true, then surely we would be able to find an account in the Bible where Jesus told someone no when asked for healing. There is not a Bible in existence today that says such a thing. It is true that not everyone in the Bible necessarily experienced healing, but this has nothing to do with Jesus not wanting to heal. It had to do with people's personal faith. As long as they were willing to come to Jesus in faith, He healed them. You or someone you know may be wondering, "Is God willing to heal me?" You might believe He chooses to heal some and not others. But the Bible says that great multitudes followed Jesus and *He healed them all*! The word *all* in Greek means all. It is time today to put an end to all doubt, skepticism, and confusion. God's unconditional will is healing. Period! You need to realize this spiritual truth deep within—God wants you healed. If you will simply accept the truth that healing is the will of God, then you will be in a position to place a faith demand on healing. Christ always manifested healing to all those who would receive it. There is no reason for anyone to teach or believe that God will only heal certain people at certain times and not heal everyone. Do not buy into the lie that is designed to rob you of what God has provided. The healing plan of God is just as firm today as it was in the beginning of creation. It is time for you to realize the loving heart of the Father toward you and receive the healing, deliverance, and restoration He has so graciously provided for us *all*.

HEALING PRAYER

Father, in the name of Jesus, I thank You for the covenant promise of healing. Your Word is not arbitrary or confusing. Your promises are forthright, and they are offered in love. Thank You for all that You desire for me. By Your grace I seek to see You as You really are, and I take Your Word as You meant it to be understood. Today I recognize it is Your perfect will to heal me. Lord, I know with my spirit man that You paid a tremendous price two thousand years ago to purchase my healing once and for all. Today I receive the finished work of the cross. I declare that healing is the children's bread and, as a covenant child of God, I receive my healing. I appropriate the promise of healing in my mind, soul, and physical body, in the name of Jesus. Amen!

Day 60

EVEN THE DOGS...

HEALING MEDITATION

*And she said, Truth, Lord: yet the dogs
eat of the crumbs which fall from their
masters' table. —Matthew 15:27*

How desperate are you to receive your healing? How far are you willing to go to see your loved ones healed? Receiving your miracle often requires desperation. No one knows more about this desperation than the Syrophoenician found in Matthew's Gospel. She came to Jesus for the express purpose of receiving healing for her daughter. To this Jesus responded with a cultural insult, "It is not meet to take the children's bread, and to cast it to dogs"

(Matthew 15:26). What would you do if you came to Jesus to be healed, and He told you that the blessing of healing did not belong to dogs? Most people would have left the church or filed a lawsuit for violating their religious and gender rights. Not this woman! She responded in the most profound way: "Yes, Lord!" She quickly agreed with God. She immediately yielded to the truth that this request was not based on her own righteousness. This was not about her religious ideology or her sin; this miracle was about the goodness of Jesus Christ. She declared, "Even the dogs eat of the crumbs which fall from their masters' table." In most of the Gospel accounts containing this story, Jesus marveled. What allowed this mother to embrace insult and rejection and continue to move toward her miracle in faith and expectation? Desperation and radical faith. These are the two elements you need in order to receive the promise of healing in your life. Too many people wear their spiritual feelings on their shoulders. If things don't look like they are going to work out the way they expect them to, they are offended. How desperate are you today? Are you so determined to receive your miracle that you are willing to press through every insult, delay, pain, and disappointment? It is time to renew your mind and posture yourself to receive the healing God has for you.

HEALING PRAYER

Father, I thank You that You love me and that through Jesus I have been given eternal access to the children's bread. Thank You for being my Healer all the days of my life. I will not fear or be afraid because I know I am secure in Your love. I am determined to receive and walk in my healing no matter what the devil says. Nothing shall separate me from Your love. I will not allow offense, hurt, or disappointment to hinder me from walking in faith and expectation. Whatever Your Word says, I believe, and Your Word declares You are good and Your mercy endures forever. Thank You, Father, for healing me in every area of my life. In Jesus's name I pray. Amen.

NO MORE EXCUSES

HEALING MEDITATION

And Jesus said unto them, Because of your unbelief: for verily I say unto you, If ye have faith as a grain of mustard seed, ye shall say unto this mountain, Remove hence to yonder place; and it shall remove; and nothing shall be impossible unto you. —Matthew 17:20

We live in a culture obsessed with excuses. We often blame our lack of education, our height, our weight, and even our ethnicity on what we can or cannot receive. I call this practice "blame shifting." Just like the man at the pool of Bethesda responded when asked by Jesus, "Will thou be made whole?" people have a tendency to eloquently express every logical explanation and excuse for why they are in their current predicament. "I have been sick a long time!" "No one will help me out!" or "The preacher hurt my feelings." Interestingly enough, none of these excuses are sufficient. Some of the aforementioned things may be factual, but it does not make them legitimate. What I love about the Word of God is that it is empowering. The more we read, study, and meditate on the Word of God, the more it will remove our excuses. There are many excuses used when it comes to healing. For instance, many people think healing depends on the severity of their condition. But Jesus said that if you have faith as a grain of mustard seed, then *nothing* shall be impossible to you. A mustard seed is the size of a grain of sand, yet it packs the potency to release God's miraculous power in our lives. Nothing shall be impossible for us if we simply believe. It does not matter what the sickness is or how long you have been diagnosed; only believe. Take the limits off of your faith. Make up in your mind that you will not tolerate any excuses. Fix your eyes on the Word of God and determine that you will accept nothing less than the Word.

HEALING PRAYER

Father, I thank You for the authority of Your Word. Through Your Word I am empowered to overcome every obstacle and limitation in my life. Your Word declares that if I have faith as of a grain of mustard seed, I will speak to the mountain and it shall be removed. By faith I speak to the mountain of sickness, disease, poverty, lack, and bondage, and I command it to be removed from me now. Nothing is impossible to be because I am a believer in Your Word. I will no longer accept any excuse because Your Word declares that I can do all things through Christ who gives me strength. I live a life of power and limitless victory through Jesus. Thank You, Lord, for a supernatural paradigm shift that causes me to increase my expectation and receive a greater manifestation of Your miraculous power. Nothing shall stand in the way of my healing in Jesus's name. Amen!

Day 62

YOU SHALL RECEIVE POWER

HEALING MEDITATION

But ye shall receive power, after that the Holy Ghost is come upon you: and ye shall be witnesses unto Me both in Jerusalem, and in all Judaea, and in Samaria, and unto the uttermost part of the earth. —Acts 1:8

What the church desperately needs in these last days is a revelation of the power of God. We serve an all-powerful God, and He has given us power to carry out His purpose and plan in the earth. Unfortunately, there is a stubborn devil who has refused to accept the rulership and government of God. He goes about putting sickness on God's people in an attempt to bring them into bondage. Jesus told His disciples to wait for the power, and after they received it they would become witnesses for Him. In order for us to be witnesses, however, we have to be able to testify of the resurrection of Jesus, which requires the demonstration of resurrection power. This power comes from the Holy Spirit. Imagine for a moment that you have unlimited power within you. Guess what? You absolutely do! You can lay hands on the sick and they shall recover—this includes laying hands on yourself. You can take authority over all the powers of darkness, including those demonic powers operating in your own life. You may not think of sickness as demonic activity, but this is how Jesus saw it. It doesn't matter whether your sickness is self-inflicted or hereditary, it's all designed to keep you from being the witness God has called you to be. Resist the devil! You have supernatural power inside you. Stop asking God to heal you; He already did that two thousand years ago. He is waiting on you and me to release the power that He has deposited within us. The time is now to deal with sickness and disease. The moment you take a stand, you will see a change. The *dynamis* power of God is operating in your spirit and is ready to manifest the healing you have been praying for in your life and the lives of your loved ones.

HEALING PRAYER

Father, I thank You for Your unlimited power working in me through the Holy Spirit. Through Your supernatural power I am equipped to be a witness. Your Word declares that I am to be filled with the Holy Spirit; therefore, I ask You to fill me afresh. I will no longer be restricted by fear, anxiety, or sin; I stand boldly in faith as a witness of the resurrection of Jesus Christ. I have explosive power on the inside of me. I release this dynamis power to affect change and lasting transformation in every area of my life. I break the power of sickness through the blood of Jesus and the Word of God, and I neutralize every attack of the enemy in my physical body. I stand victorious as an ambassador of the kingdom of God on the earth. Thank You for my freedom. In Jesus's name I pray, amen!

Day 63

RECEIVING STRENGTH

HEALING MEDITATION

That He would grant you, according to the riches
of His glory, to be strengthened with might by
His Spirit in the inner man. —Ephesians 3:16

In the book of Acts, while Peter and John went up to the temple to pray, they encountered a man who was crippled from his mother's womb. Like most of the physically handicapped people of that time, he was asking for alms. Peter looked at him and said, "Silver and gold have I none; but such as I have give I thee: in the name of Jesus Christ of Nazareth rise up and walk." Then in the next verse it says, "And he took him by the right hand,

and lifted him up: and immediately his feet and ankle bones received strength" (Acts 3:6-7) This was a wonderful miracle to say the least. However, there is an aspect to this miracle that is very important when discussing divine healing. When the apostle Peter took the impotent man by the hand, the Bible says "immediately his feet and ankle bones received strength." The word *strength* in this passage is the Greek word *stereoō*, which means "to make firm, to make solid, and to strengthen" (Strong's, G4732). This was not just a physical strength but a spiritual empowerment. God was addressing the whole man through this miracle of healing. He was restoring, repairing, and reestablishing this man from the inside out. He received something that changed him. Now he was able to praise God and fulfill his purpose in life. He was able to walk and function the way God always intended for him. This is God's entire agenda in healing and/or delivering us. He desires to restore the internal infrastructure that has been torn down through sickness and oppression. God wants to strengthen your inner man by His Spirit. Once your inner man is strengthened, your physical man has no choice but to follow behind. May you be strengthened with might by His Spirit in your inward man so that you can worship the Lord freely.

HEALING PRAYER

Father, in the name of Your Son Jesus, I thank You for Your great love for me. I pray that You would grant me, according to the riches of Your glory, a revelation of Your power working in me. I declare that I am strengthened with might by Your Spirit in my inner man. I receive strength in every area of my spirit, soul, and body in Jesus's name. I declare that I am made firm and solid by Your Word. My foundation is built upon the rock of Your Word, not my feelings or emotions. Therefore, healing, deliverance, and restoration belong to me, and any sickness or infirmity must leave my body. Thank You, Father, for addressing my whole man through Your miracle of healing. Everyone I know will be healed because of Your supernatural power working within me. In the name of Jesus I pray, amen!

SAY NO TO OFFENSE

HEALING MEDITATION

Let all bitterness, and wrath, and anger, and clamour, and evil speaking, be put away from you, with all malice: and be ye kind one to another, tenderhearted, forgiving one another, even as God for Christ's sake hath forgiven you. —Ephesians 4:31-32

We are commanded by God to refrain from offense and bitterness. Real faith is always demonstrated through our obedience. Without obedience to the Word of God, what we call faith may instead just be religious jargon. We cannot say we trust God for our healing when we are walking around resenting people. How do you know when you have offense in your heart? The word *offense* comes from the Greek word *skandalon*, meaning a trap (Strong's, G4625). When you are unable to fellowship, pray for, or love on people freely, then this is a sign you have fallen into the trap of offense. Essentially, offense is any thing that causes us to distrust another person, stumble, or fall away from relationship. God knows that offense, anger, and bitterness open the door to demonic activity in our lives, including sickness and disease. I know firsthand the devastating effects resentment and offense can have on the body. I remember a time when I was unknowingly harboring offense in my heart and my body was suffering as a result of it. In fact, there are specific ailments and diseases I believe are directly connected to offense, such as arthritis, gout, autoimmune disorders, cancer, diabetes, and skin disorders. We have seen many healed as they have released those who have deeply wounded them. Why does the devil want you offended? The enemy of your soul wants you sick, bound, and unable to fulfill your kingdom assignment, and he uses offense to accomplish this purpose. Today you need to make a conscious and deliberate effort to forgive. The Holy Spirit has already endowed you with the power to forgive, so don't fall into the trap of Satan! You deserve to be healed and whole, and you should not settle for anything less.

HEALING PRAYER

Father, in the name of Jesus Christ, I thank You for the blood of Jesus that was shed on the cross for my sins. I thank You for the work of redemption that brought about my healing according to 1 Peter 2:24. I freely forgive all those who have wounded or offended me. I release all my debtors as an act of my free will. Lord, through Your grace I receive complete restoration in Jesus's name. I refuse to be offended from this day forward. Holy Spirit, I ask that You act as a supernatural gatekeeper, guarding my heart from any and all offense. I declare that I am released from the bait and snare of Satan, and I adopt the mentality of radical forgiveness. I choose to give and receive love freely, without any restriction.

Day 65

DESTROYING THE YOKE

HEALING MEDITATION

And it shall come to pass in that day, that his burden shall be taken away from off thy shoulder, and his yoke from off thy neck, and the yoke shall be destroyed because of the anointing. —Isaiah 10:27

In the book of Luke, Jesus goes into the synagogue (as was His custom) and He began to read from the scroll (in Isaiah 61) where it says, "The Spirit of the Lord is upon Me, because He hath anointed Me to preach the gospel to the poor; He hath sent Me to heal the brokenhearted, to preach deliverance to the captives, and recovering of sight to the blind, to set at liberty them that are bruised, to preach the acceptable year of the Lord" (Luke 4:18-19). This was the fulfillment of a Messianic prophecy. Through Adam's transgression, Satan placed a yoke of bondage upon mankind, consisting of sickness, poverty, and death. Have you seen sickness as a yoke of bondage? This is exactly what it is! First John 3:8 says, "For this purpose the Son of God was manifested, that He might destroy the works of the devil." Jesus came to destroy the yoke Satan placed upon God's people, particularly sickness and disease. Notice the Bible says He came to "destroy," which is the Greek word *lyō*, meaning to unbind, dissolve, and deprive of authority (Strong's, G3089). Jesus unbound us, dissolved the chains of captivity over us, and deprived the enemy of all authority in our lives through the cross. Now we have to walk as those who have been made free. You no longer need to live in bondage to sin or sickness. Aren't you glad that you serve a God who would give so much of Himself just so that you could experience the freedom and victory He purposed from the very beginning? Whenever you are confronted with sickness or disease in your life or the life of someone you love, remind yourself that Jesus already destroyed the yoke of sickness. And He will continue to destroy yokes of bondage so long as you believe.

HEALING PRAYER

Father, in the name of Jesus, I thank You that the Son of God was manifested to destroy the works of the devil. Sickness is a work of the devil; therefore, I loose myself from the bondage of sickness and infirmity in all of its forms and expressions. From this day forward I declare that I am one with You, Lord Jesus, and through Your shed blood I am forgiven of all sin and released from all bondage. I renounce the curse of sickness, poverty, and death, and I command any and all demonic activity to cease operation in my life today. Your Word says that perfect love casts out fear. So in the name of Jesus I command all fear to leave me now. I will no longer toil or struggle for my freedom, but I will walk in effortless victory and success in You. In Jesus's name I ask these things, amen!

NATURAL VERSUS SPIRITUAL

HEALING MEDITATION

But the natural man receiveth not the things of the Spirit of God: for they are foolishness unto him: neither can he know them, because they are spiritually discerned. —1 Corinthians 2:14

There is a significant difference between the natural and the spiritual. And many believers are ignorant of this reality. This becomes even more evident when it comes to healing, because healing is first and foremost a spiritual reality, a result of the redemptive work of Christ. The Bible says that in our natural state we do not receive the things of God, because they are foolishness to the natural mind. If you tell a person who is not born again, and who is confined to a hospital bed, they are already healed, you will encounter confusion or even hostility. The truth is that the Word of God was never intended to appeal to the natural man. The Word of God is spiritual; therefore, we must approach God's Word with spiritual understanding. By natural, we are referring to the sensual nature governed by the five senses. The natural realm is governed by the feelings, thoughts, emotions, and in response to what we can see or touch. When the doctor issues an evil report, the natural mind receives it as truth because of the apparent credibility of its source; however, the spiritual mind knows better. Through spiritual discernment we are able to see what God has done for us and is currently doing. By "spiritual discernment" I am referring to the ability to examine or judge things to determine whether they are true or false. We know healing is a finished work no matter what the doctor's report says. Discernment allows us to see the truth of the Word rather than the lie of the enemy. The good news is that you are no longer governed by the natural realm. The moment you gave your life to Christ, you became governed by the spiritual. What seems like foolishness to the world should make perfect sense to you. Stop trying to rationalize your healing; there is nothing rational about divine healing. Healing will often violate the very laws of nature itself. All you need to do is receive your healing by faith in the Word of God.

HEALING PRAYER

Father, in the name of Jesus, I thank You for who You are and all that You have done. Through Your Spirit I am able to discern what is from You and what is not from You. I am not a natural man; I am a spiritual man. I declare that I am no longer ruled by my senses, but I am ruled by the Word of God as the final authority in my life. Thank You for the ability to hear Your voice and to think according to Your Word. I have the mind of Christ and the faith of Christ. When I am faced with symptoms or attacks in my body, I will align my faith and my thought life with the truth of Your Word. The Word of God is my reality. I will only subscribe to the report of the Lord. No matter what I feel, see, or hear, I know what Your Word says is the only truth I believe. In the name of Jesus I pray. Amen!

Day 67

WALK IN THE SPIRIT

HEALING MEDITATION

This I say then, Walk in the Spirit, and ye shall not fulfil the lust of the flesh. —Galatians 5:16

Since I was a young child, I have heard the expression, "Walk in the Spirit." You may have heard this expression in church or other religious settings as well. What does it mean to walk in the Spirit? There are many different perspectives on this passage, but I believe that to walk in the Spirit simply means to walk according to the Word of God as opposed to anything else in life. It means to follow the leading of the Holy Spirit. This means that we are to see things from God's vantage point and respond to things based on the Word of God. Our flesh represents the carnal man, which is the place where indwelling sin and the law rule and reign. For example, when a person is diagnosed with a chronic or terminal illness, their first thought is usually, "What did I do to deserve this?" or "God must be trying to teach me a lesson!" Instead of seeing the diagnosis as an overt attack of the evil one, they take it personally and find themselves unable to exercise the faith necessary to "quench the fiery darts" of the devil. They are actually walking in the flesh. Our flesh longs to be comforted, satisfied, and even worshiped. I have found that there are many people who do not want to be healed. Why? They are in the flesh. They are more interested in the attention, comfort, and even financial remuneration they receive from being sick than the blessing of being healed. When we are walking in the Spirit, we are functioning according to the Word of God. The Bible promises that when we are walking in the Spirit, we will not fulfill the lust or desires of the flesh. The flesh is diametrically opposed to the Spirit. This is why you cannot be in faith and fear simultaneously. It is a spiritual contradiction. Make the decision to walk in the Spirit, to walk by faith, and be empowered. The devil may have told you that things will never get better; but it's a lie! Put off the flesh and embrace the Spirit today.

HEALING PRAYER

Father, in the name of Jesus, I thank You that I walk in the Spirit and not in the flesh. Thank You for victory over the works of the flesh. I choose today to be led by the Holy Spirit in every area of my life. Help me to identify the flesh when it is operating, and thank You for the power of the indwelling Spirit to overcome. I declare that Your Word is true, regardless of situations and circumstances to the contrary. I delight in Your Word, and through my connection to You I bare eternal fruit for Your glory. Your Word says that where the Spirit of the Lord is there is liberty; so thank You for liberty. I choose to reject every lie of the devil. I choose to walk in divine health because it pleases You. From this day forward I walk in the Spirit and not in the flesh in Jesus's name.

GOD'S DIVINE RECIPE

And it came to pass on a certain day, as He was teaching, that there were Pharisees and doctors of the law sitting by, which were come out of every town of Galilee, and Judaea, and Jerusalem: and the power of the Lord was present to heal them. —Luke 5:17

I really enjoy cooking. The key to cooking is to have a really good recipe. Recipes are the means by which we combine ingredients to create a dish pleasing to the senses. Jesus was the Anointed One "who went about doing good and healing all those who were oppressed of the devil" (Acts 10:38). God has revealed to us His divine recipe—the power, the will, and the source of healing. Jesus applied these ingredients together during His earthly ministry to see the sick healed and the dead raised. If we apply these truths to our lives, we will be confident that God is able to heal us, and we will be well supplied with the grace to walk in this reality. The main ingredient to this "divine recipe" is the power of the Holy Spirit. Jesus was teaching on a certain day and He sensed that the power of God was present, which was the perfect ingredient for healing to take place. This same power is present today. In addition to the power of God being available to us, there is the simple fact that Jesus died on the cross, defeated Satan, and rose again on the third day to bring us to a place where we could walk in the covenant blessing of divine healing. The same Spirit that raised Jesus Christ from the dead dwells on the inside of us (see Romans 8:11). The anointing that was upon Jesus, healing the sick and raising the dead, is the same anointing that is on the inside of each and every one of us (see 1 John 2:27). We know that God is the Healer because Christ is the Healer, and the Father and Son are one. We also know that we have all the tools we need to make divine healing and health realities in our lives right now! The key is to mix our faith with His power.

HEALING PRAYER

Thank You, Father, for revealing the aspects of healing demonstrated in Jesus's earthly ministry. I believe the record of Your Word. I know You have the power to heal every sickness and disease. I am so grateful to know it is Your desire to heal all who are sick. And I know that the source of healing power is the Holy Spirit. Thank You for revealing Your nature and ways so I can resist the works of darkness in my life and in the lives of others! Today I will combine this "divine recipe" in order to see the manifestation of divine healing in my life and in the lives of my loved ones. There is no difference from the anointing that was on Jesus and the anointing that dwells in me. I recognize that the power of God is present to heal right now. No longer will I be a victim to sickness and disease, but I will release the power operating in me by the Holy Spirit. In Jesus's name I pray. Amen.

Day 69

WHAT DO YOU EXPECT?

HEALING MEDITATION

*And he gave heed unto them, expecting to
receive something of them.* —Acts 3:5

What are you expecting from God today? Our expectation is very powerful when it comes to receiving healing. In fact, the attitude of expectation is the atmosphere for the miraculous. I often tell people that what they set their mind upon will ultimately manifest in their lives. What is your mind set upon today? Do you believe God to receive the manifestation of your healing today? In the Bible you will often see that Jesus would tell people, "According to your faith, be it unto you." We have been taught by religion and tradition that God will do certain things if it is "His will." This is not what the Bible teaches. In fact, we have to place a demand on God through faith and expectation. We are not to just passively sit and wait for God to do something. The Bible says we are saved by hope (see Romans 8:24). The word *hope* means "confident expectation of good." This confident expectation produces deliverance in our lives. Just as the impotent beggar gazed upon Peter and John, expecting to receive something from them, so we must expect from God. That impotent man received much more than he ever bargained for. To expect means to look for something. Are you looking actively for your miracle? Every day you need to charge your expectation with the Word of God. The more you think on the Word, the more your faith will increase; and the more your faith increases, the more your expectation will increase. Soon you will attract everything you expect. Everyone has expectation. The question remains: What are you expecting? There are some people who always expect to be disappointed. They never come for prayer or grab onto the Word because they have convinced themselves they will ultimately be disappointed. Beloved, this is not the right attitude to have. Be careful not to fall into the trap of negative expectation. Make up your mind that you will expect nothing less than what God has promised you in His Word. I guarantee your expectation will not be disappointed.

HEALING PRAYER

Father, I thank You that Your Word promises that my expectation will not be disappointed. You said that if I will ask anything in Your name, believing, I will certainly receive. I stand on the promise of Your Word concerning health and healing, and I declare that I am already healed from the crown of my head to the soles of my feet. Every fiber of my being receives supernatural strength this very moment. Your Word declares that I am saved by confident expectation, and right now I confidently expect Your promise of deliverance and wholeness in my life. Thank You for healing me. Thank You for delivering me from the snare of the enemy. Thank You for making me whole in You. From this day forward I will confidently expect miracles at every turn. Nothing is impossible for me because I am a believer of Your Word. In Jesus's name I ask, amen.

Day 70

SO MUCH MORE!

*Jesus saith unto her, Said I not unto thee,
that, if thou wouldest believe, thou shouldest
see the glory of God?* —John 11:40

One of my favorite stories in the Gospels is the story of Lazarus, the brother of Mary and Martha. This story has the ultimate happy ending—a man who was sick and eventually died was raised from the dead. Oh how marvelous is our Savior! The irony of the story is that Jesus waited for Lazarus to die. Technically, He could have healed him before he died; yet He waited patiently for his death. What was the purpose of this? There are so many people today who are sick, bound, and even angry with God for the things He has "allowed" in their lives. Many have found themselves in the same place, praying for change but to no avail. Like the sisters of Lazarus, they don't believe things can get any better. In the book of John, Jesus has a profound conversation with Martha (the sister of Lazarus). He commands the stone over Lazarus's tomb to be taken away. To this Martha objects. Then Jesus said to her, "Said I not unto thee, that, if thou wouldest believe, thou shouldest see the glory of God?" He reminded her that this was not the end, it was just the beginning. Where she was ready to give up, Jesus was just showing up. I don't know where you are today, but I want to remind you that this is not the end. There is so much more! The glory of God is yet to be revealed. Don't stop believing. You have been crying out for more and God wants to give you just that. There is always frustration before manifestation. Do you want more from the Lord? Are you ready to live the life He intends for you? The choice is yours! You can weep and mourn, or you can "roll away" the stone in faith and expectation with the realization that there is so much more that God wants to reveal. He wants to show you there is nothing He cannot handle, there is no sickness He cannot heal, and no bondage He is incapable of breaking. Open your heart to more of Him today.

HEALING PRAYER

Father, in the name of Jesus, I thank You for being the God of resurrection. There is nothing impossible for You. From the beginning of creation, You have revealed Your plan of redemption and restoration for us. Thank You for creating in me a desire for more of You; not that You have withheld Yourself from me or restricted Your power, but I want to yield to You more than I have. Through You dead things are brought to life again. I refuse to surrender to the lies of the enemy; instead, I move forward in bold faith and confidence and assurance, knowing that Your Word will never fail. I believe there is more to the Christian life than unanswered prayer and defeat—there is a life of power, love, and victory. I choose to embrace them today. In the name of Jesus I pray, amen.

Day 71

SOWING AND REAPING

Be not deceived; God is not mocked: for whatsoever a man soweth, that shall he also reap. For he that soweth to his flesh shall of the flesh reap corruption; but he that soweth to the Spirit shall of the Spirit reap life everlasting. —Galatians 6:7-8

One of the most important laws in the kingdom of God is the law of sowing and reaping. By calling it a law, we mean a principle or precept. This is the means by which God governs and administers His system of blessing. In fact, the Bible says, "While the earth remaineth, seedtime and harvest, and cold and heat, and summer and winter, and day and night shall not cease" (Genesis 8:22). This means it is an irrevocable reality. Unfortunately, it is a reality many believers seem to ignore. For example, our words are seeds; yet there are people who speak words of doubt, fear, death, and condemnation while at the same time hoping for a favorable outcome. It is impossible! The Bible says we should not be deceived, for whatever we sow we will reap. Do you believe this? The Bible goes even further to say that if we sow to the flesh we will reap corruption. What does it mean to sow to the flesh? It means we invest time, words, energy, and resources to that which is contrary to the Word of God. Remember, the harvest we reap is exponential to the seed sown. In other words, you don't sow an apple seed and get one apple; you reap an apple tree. In the same token, if we want to reap the exponential manifestation of healing in our lives, we must sow seeds of healing. What are the seeds of healing? Prayer, faith, and the Word of God. The more you engage in these things, the more you are sowing life-giving seeds that will ultimately result in you receiving your healing (in an exponential measure). This is what it means to sow to the Spirit. On the other hand, to sow to the flesh means to sow seeds of fear, doubt, and negative words; these things will ultimately produce corruption, or destruction and decay. If there is destruction and decay in your life, it is time to examine the seeds you have sown, and, if necessary, speak crop failure to them. Today is the day to sow "good seeds" and you will eventually reap a harvest of healing, health, and wholeness.

HEALING PRAYER

Father, in the name of Jesus, I speak crop failure to every bad seed I have sown with my thoughts, words, or actions. I know You are the Lord of the harvest and that You only desire good for my life. Today I make the conscious decision to sow the seed of the Word of God into my spirit and speak life to every part of my being. You have a goodly heritage for me and life is fertile soil for Your blessing and provision. I reap the exponential harvest of health and healing through the power of Your Word operating in me. I declare that I will no longer sow to the flesh, but I will consciously and intentionally sow to the Spirit, reaping life. In Jesus's name I pray. Amen!

Day 72

TIME STAND STILL!

Then spake Joshua to the Lord in the day when the Lord delivered up the Amorites before the children of Israel, and he said in the sight of Israel, Sun, stand thou still upon Gibeon; and thou, Moon, in the valley of Ajalon. —Joshua 10:12-14

In the beginning of creation, God set the sun and the moon as the means of separating day from night and regulating the seasons (see Genesis 1:14-18). The sun serves as the "greater light" and is the measurement of time till today. During the Bible days, however, there was no electricity so all work had to be done, all wars had to be fought, and all travel took place during the daytime. As you can see, the sun was a huge deal. In the book of Joshua, as the Israelites were battling the Amorites, Joshua commanded the sun and the moon to stand still. This is what many call the "long day" miracle. Essentially, Joshua was commanding time itself to stand still. Why was this so important? If the night fell, they would no longer be able to conquer their enemies. Time poses a challenge for many believers. You may have been given a prognosis or a deadline. Time tends to agitate your struggles. In fact, the word for "be thou still" is the Hebrew word *damam* and it means to be silent, still, or dumbstruck (Strong's, H1826). We get countless prayer requests from people who have been suffering from an ailment or an addiction for years. Like Joshua, they feel like the enemy is closing in on them and they are running out of time. I want to remind you of something: You serve a God who can do the impossible. He loves you so much that He is willing to suspend time on your behalf. If God will cause the sun and moon to stand still for the children of Israel, what won't He do for you? You too can speak to the circumstances of your life and command them to "stand still." You can command your trials to be silent. All it takes is faith and audacity. Remind yourself that you have a covenant with God. Time now works for you and not against you! Today is the day of your victory.

HEALING PRAYER

Father, in the name of Jesus Christ, I thank You that nothing is impossible to him that believes. I am a believer of Your Word and not a doubter. Whatever I ask in faith, believing, I shall receive. Right now, I boldly declare that I have audacious faith. I speak to the circumstances of my life and command them to be silenced by the power of Almighty God. I command every evil report to become deaf and dumb in the name of Jesus. No weapon formed against me shall prosper and every tongue that rises against me in judgment is condemned. Thank You, Lord, for being my miracle worker. I rejoice in Your might. Today I will see victory over the enemy. In Jesus's name, amen!

Day 73

LESSONS FROM BARTIMAEUS

HEALING MEDITATION

And they came to Jericho: and as He went out of Jericho with His disciples and a great number of people, blind Bartimaeus, the son of Timaeus, sat by the highway side begging. And when he heard that it was Jesus of Nazareth, he began to cry out, and say, Jesus, Thou Son of David, have mercy on me. —Mark 10:46-47

In the Bible, Jesus indicted the Pharisees and religious leaders of His day, suggesting they were "the blind leading the blind." However, there is one instance in the Bible where a blind man teaches us a great deal about Jesus and healing. Jesus encountered a man by the name of Bartimaeus. He was a typical blind beggar in the city of Jericho (they were quite common in Israel). The Bible says that when he heard that it was Jesus of Nazareth passing by, he cried out, "Jesus, Thou Son of David, have mercy on me." Why did this man cry out in this manner? He recognized who Jesus was and he responded accordingly. I wish more of us would recognize who Jesus is and respond accordingly; if we did we would see His miraculous power demonstrated in ways we can't imagine. Jesus longs to demonstrate His compassion for us through healing. Bartimaeus refused to remain in his situation, and when he saw a way out of his struggle, he took it. There are countless people today who are simply content in their sickness. They have become comfortable in that state. Many of them will actually become hostile when you suggest to them that God wants them healed. We need to be like Bartimaeus, in the sense that he refused to remain silent when Jesus was near. Everything around him was telling him to keep quiet, but the more these things attempted to silence him, the louder he became. In the end, Jesus called him and asked him what He should do for him. Bartimaeus requested his sight. To this request Jesus said, "Go thy way; thy faith hath made thee whole. And immediately he received his sight, and followed Jesus in the way" (Mark 10:52).

HEALING PRAYER

Father, in the name of Jesus, I thank You for being a God of great compassion and love. You are my Healer and Redeemer. Today I call upon You to deliver me from any and all affliction in my life. I realize that Your healing power working in me is not based on my own works or goodness, but is based on who You are. You are the Healer. I refuse to be confined to my limitations or fears; instead, I choose to receive all You have provided for me. I command every demon to be silent in the name of Jesus. I am determined to receive my healing, and I will extend beyond my comfort to receive it. Thank You, Lord, that from today on my life will never be the same again. In the name of Jesus I pray, amen!

Day 74

HIS GRACE IS SUFFICIENT

HEALING MEDITATION

And He said unto me, My grace is sufficient
for thee: for My strength is made perfect in
weakness. Most gladly therefore will I rather
glory in my infirmities, that the power of Christ
may rest upon me. —2 Corinthians 12:9

Have you ever heard the expression, "My thorn in the flesh"? The first time I heard it, the context of this statement was referring to sickness and disease. In other words, the person was suggesting that God gave them this sickness as a means to humble and teach them. I heard it often and even started to believe it myself until I read the

Bible. I have said before and will continue to affirm it: Our faith must be based on the Word of God alone. Paul cried out to God because of a difficulty in his life. He continually asked God to remove it from him, but God said, "My grace is sufficient for thee: for My strength is made perfect in weakness." The word *grace* in this passage is the Greek word *charis*, and it means "enabling power" or "supernatural ability" (Strong's, G5485). The truth is that God already gave Paul everything he needed to overcome every challenge before him. He had everything he needed inside of him to address the attacks of Satan. By the way, this in no way suggests God gave this affliction to Paul or that Paul was bound by sickness or disease, but it does tell us that he was being afflicted by something. The Bible gives us the solution to this affliction—the grace and power of God. We have already been given everything we need to overcome. We don't need to wait on God to answer our prayers; He is waiting on us to move in faith and authority, and to place a demand on what He has already accomplished on the cross. Stop behaving like a victim; I repeat, stop behaving like a victim! You are powerful because greater is He that lives in you than he that lives in the world. The very power of Christ rests upon you in your infirmities.

HEALING PRAYER

Father, I thank You that every promise in Your Word is yes and amen. Your Word is clear and uncomplicated; You love me and have a good plan for my life. You desire that I be healed. I accept healing so that I will be able to live out Your perfect will for my life. Today, in Jesus's name, I accept Your supernatural grace available to me. Your grace empowers me to stand in the midst of spiritual, mental, physical, and emotional weakness. Your grace is sufficient for me in every area of my life. I now hold up the shield of faith to quench all of the fiery darts of the evil one, in the name of Jesus. Thank You, Lord, for Your love for me. In Jesus's name I pray, amen!

Day 75

BE DOERS OF THE WORD

But be ye doers of the word, and not hearers only, deceiving your own selves. —James 1:22

Confessing the Word of God is a very powerful means to see the promises of God realized in your life. But the truth of the matter is that it is not enough to confess the Word—we must be doers of the Word as well. There are three aspects to walking in divine healing. First, you have to hear the Word of God. The Bible says that faith comes by hearing and hearing by the Word of God (see Romans 10:17). The hearing the Bible is talking about is the Greek word *akoē*, and it means to exercise the sense (spiritual sense) of hearing (Strong's, G189). This takes place when the Holy Spirit breathes life on the Word inside your spirit. Once you have heard the Word, the next thing is to believe the Word. To believe simply means to accept it as true. The first act of believing is speaking. Paul says in 2 Corinthians 4:13, "We also believe, and therefore speak." Speaking is the natural consequence of believing. Jesus declared that out of the "abundance of the heart [the] mouth speaketh" (Luke 6:45). After we have heard and believed, the next and most critical step is to act on what we believe. Simply put, we must be doers of the Word. What does it mean to be a doer of the Word? To "do" means to perform, obey, and fulfill it. I often hear people say, "I believe the Word!" The question is not whether you believe it or not, but whether you are doing what you say you believe. If a man said he was the greatest rock climber in the world, yet he refused to climb a single rock, wouldn't you question his belief? What we say is worthless if it is not followed by consistent action. In the case of healing, you have to do what your faith and confession dictates. If you are believing for your healing, do something you couldn't do before. Move on your faith until you see the manifestation. Stop waiting on something to happen. Be a doer of the Word today!

HEALING PRAYER

Father, in the name of Jesus Christ, I come to You in faith and expectation, knowing that You are a good God, and that it is impossible for You to lie. Today I declare that I am a believer and not a doubter. From this day forward I declare that I am a doer of the Word. I am Your sheep and I hear Your voice, and a stranger I will not follow. It is my delight to keep Your commands and to execute them daily. Day and night I meditate on Your Word and look for opportunities to demonstrate that Word. Thank You for creating in me a heart that desires to seek You and please You in every area of my life. I will perform, obey, and fulfill every Word You speak to me. In Jesus's name I pray. Amen!

GOD SHALL BRUISE SATAN

HEALING MEDITATION

And the God of peace shall bruise Satan under your feet shortly. The grace of our Lord Jesus Christ be with you. Amen. —Romans 16:20

The simple truth is that you and I are fighting a defeated foe. What does this mean? It means that Jesus Christ has already won. Satan is angry that he has but a short time on this earth to carry out his chaotic plan, and he knows that this plan will not prevail. This is why he attempts to afflict the body of Christ with sickness, disease, poverty, and even death if possible. The good news is that God has given us authority over the devil. We don't have to yield to his demonic activity in our lives or the lives of others any longer. The even greater news is that God has promised that He will bruise Satan under our feet shortly. Notice the Bible did not say that God will bruise Satan under *His* feet; He said Satan will be bruised under *our* feet. The word *bruise* means to break in pieces. Isn't that good news? God says that in a little while He is going to break the enemy in pieces under your feet. Remember, God is a God of peace and justice. He takes no pleasure in the affliction of His people. He sees what you have been dealing with and it angers Him more than it angers you. Make no mistake about it: God will vindicate the oppression of the devil. In the meantime, you have everything you need to deal with the enemy. You no longer have to allow him to operate unhindered in your family, your church, or your community. I call this "holding the devil accountable." As a representative of Jesus Christ on earth, you have been charged with the responsibility of "policing the earth," and when you see something that violates God's law, you ought to address it. Put the devil under your feet, right where he belongs.

HEALING PRAYER

Father, in the name of Jesus, I thank You for the authority that You have given me. Through this authority and power, I command any and all satanic activity in my thoughts, emotions, mind, or body to cease and desist. Based on Your Word, I no longer tolerate sickness or disease. I declare that sickness is a criminal, and through the authority vested in me by Jesus Christ, I arrest the criminals of sickness, disease, and oppression. Thank You, Father, for being the God of all justice and peace. I declare that Satan is defeated and placed underneath my feet, right where he belongs. Thank You that he is bruised, crushed, broken, and destroyed out of my life and out of my family line. Sickness, I serve you notice that you no longer have the legal right to operate. From this day forward you are a trespasser, in Jesus's name. Amen!

Day 77

LORD, HAVE MERCY!

*And, behold, a woman of Canaan came
out of the same coasts, and cried unto Him,
saying, Have mercy on me, O Lord, Thou
Son of David; my daughter is grievously
vexed with a devil.* —Matthew 15:22

When it comes to healing (and everything else in the Christian life), it is important to know the character of God. The way you perceive God will determine how you approach Him, especially in times of great trial and difficulty. Many people see God as a cruel tyrant who lies in wait for unsuspecting victims, punishing them when they least expect it. The church is partly responsible for this mindset being propagated. We have taught that God loves to punish sinners and evildoers. Unfortunately, even when it comes to prophecy, we somehow have been convinced that every tornado or natural disaster is a judgment of God against some marginalized group of people. I am sorry to burst your theological bubble, but God is depicted much differently than that in the Bible. The Bible says in John 14:9, "Jesus saith unto him, Have I been so long time with you, and yet hast thou not known Me, Philip? he that hath seen Me hath seen the Father; and how sayest thou then, Shew us the Father?" What does this mean? It means that Jesus is the express image of God the Father. If we want an accurate picture of the Father, we should look at His Son Jesus. All throughout the Gospels, Jesus goes about healing those who are sick, raising the dead, and casting out demons as a manifestation of the kingdom of God. Jesus does not reflect a religious tyrant that we have been indoctrinated to embrace. Instead, Jesus reveals a God of mercy and compassion, a God who longs to heal and restore His people. Mercy means that He withholds judgment or shows compassion. This is masterfully illustrated in Matthew where Jesus heals a Canaanite woman. She was not deserving of healing or deliverance, but Jesus healed her because God is good and she believed.

HEALING PRAYER

Father, I thank You that You are a good God. You are a God of mercy and compassion. I recognize that You are also a God of justice, but Your ultimate desire is to restore me and heal me. Thank You, Lord, for saving me. Through Your Son Jesus I have a clearer picture of who You are and what Your will is concerning my life. The devil is the one who wants to kill, steal, and destroy. You are the One who has come that I might have life and have it in abundance. Right now, I receive Your unconditional love and forgiveness by faith. I declare that I will never mischaracterize You again. Thank You, Lord, for having mercy on me. I pray these things in Jesus's name, amen!

Day 78

TRUST IN THE LORD

Trust in the Lord with all thine heart; and lean not unto thine own understanding. —Proverbs 3:5

We know from the Bible that faith is a large part of our ability to receive anything from God, especially when it comes to healing. Many people have taught on the principle of faith, some more clearly than others. Faith is simply confidence in the Word of God. However, the Bible tells us that we ought to trust the Lord. Trust goes even deeper than faith in the sense that trust implies complete reliance and dependency on someone else. It comes from the Hebrew word *batach*, and it means to be confident and secure (Strong's, H982). God wants us to be confident and secure in Him. This is more than just faith in His ability, but it transcends to trust in His character. When you know who God is, then you know He always has a good outcome in mind for you. Trusting the character of God is essential to being able to receive healing. God is the Healer! He always heals—this we can be confident in. God does not change; He remains consistent. That is the reason we can trust Him. To trust Him, we must lean on His Word rather than our own understanding. Many times when people believe God for their healing, they fall into the trap of depending on their own understanding or logic. Beloved, we don't need to lean on our understanding because God has already figured everything out. Stop racking your brain trying to figure out who, what, when, where, and how. The answer to all of those questions are the same anyway—God! He has it under control. He will hasten to perform His Word. He will never leave you nor forsake you. There is no need to worry or be afraid. Trust in the Lord with all your heart today.

HEALING PRAYER

Father, in the name of Jesus, I thank You for Your great love toward me. I trust You, Lord, with all my heart and I don't lean on my own understanding. In all my ways, I choose to acknowledge You. Thank You, Lord, that through Your grace and power I am able to face tomorrow and conquer every obstacle before me. I know You are a good God all of the time; therefore, I know that I can confidently follow Your leading wherever You choose to lead me. I declare in the name of Jesus that all forms of oppression I have embraced consciously or unconsciously are null and void. Father, thank You for Your Word because it is trustworthy and true; I have confidence in it. I stand upon the substance and substructure of Your Word, convinced that all You have promised has already been accomplished through the finished work of the cross of Christ. I take Your Word to heart— thank You for showing me how I should act on it. I place a demand today upon that finished work, fully expecting to see it manifested in every area of my life. In Jesus's name I ask, amen.

Day 79

LIFE MORE ABUNDANTLY

HEALING MEDITATION

The thief cometh not, but for to steal, and to kill, and to destroy: I am come that they might have life, and that they might have it more abundantly. —John 10:10

Jesus came so that you and I could have the abundant life. What does the abundant life look like? I can tell you that it does not look like sickness and disease. In fact, as a young person growing up in the church, I was actually confused. I would hear songs like, "You're the God Who Heals Me," yet when I looked around, so many people were sick. They weren't happy in their sickness either.

I believe the enemy has attempted to get the church to embrace a life that is beneath the perfect will of our heavenly Father. The question remains: What does it mean to have abundant life? Jesus explained to the disciples that He came that we might have "life." This is the Greek word *zoe,* meaning "the same quality of life God has in Himself" (Strong's, G2222). This is eternal life or unfailing life. When is the last time God took a sick day or struggled with high blood pressure? This Scripture is offensive, for it is meant to offend our complacency. God does not want us to settle for less than what He has ordained for us. This *zoe* life is all-encompassing; it affects our spirit, soul, and body. This includes healing of any and all diseases and walking in consistent divine health. The word for *more abundantly* means "filled to the full, till it overflows." Is your life filled to the full until it overflows? The good news is that it doesn't matter how your life has been up to this point; today is a new day! You can begin again. All you have to do is place your faith and trust in Jesus, and His life will become your life. Whether you have been a Christian for some time or you are new to the things of God, it does not matter. Embrace the life God has for you today. You don't have to stay sick. You don't have to stay depressed. The life of God is flowing inside of you now and you are destined for victory.

HEALING PRAYER

Father, I declare that there is only one truth: Your Word. Your Word declares that You came that I might have life and have it more abundantly. I declare that the zoe life of God flows through the very fiber of my being, in the name of Jesus. Sickness cannot stay in my body any longer because of Your eternal life working in and through me. I acknowledge Your holy Word as the highest and final authority in my life. I declare that all of my feelings and emotions must bow to Your Word. I am not motivated by what I see, hear, or feel; I am only motivated by the Word of God. I recognize that Your Word is Your will for my life. I can rely on Your Word for anything that pertains to me. I embrace health and healing as a way of life. Miracles are commonplace to me and the power of God flows through me constantly because I am a conduit of heaven. I am no longer controlled by my external circumstances, but by Your Word. In Jesus's name I pray, amen.

Day 80

YOUR BODY IS BLESSED

HEALING MEDITATION

And ye shall serve the Lord your God, and
He shall bless thy bread, and thy water; and
I will take sickness away from the midst of
thee. There shall nothing cast their young,
nor be barren, in thy land: the number of thy
days I will fulfil. —Exodus 23:25-26

Several years ago I got hold of the truth that healing was a covenant God made with His people and ratified through Jesus Christ. I came to understand I had a right to be healed; I had a right to be delivered. It was difficult to accept at first, because it meant I would have to shift my paradigm and rid myself of excuses. And that sort of process can be very uncomfortable. Nonetheless, God engraved this truth deep within the recesses of my heart. There was a married couple who came to us for ministry one day not too long ago. They were expecting a new baby, yet the husband was very disillusioned. Prior to this pregnancy they had a miscarriage, which was devastating for the couple; but the husband took it especially hard. He was so devastated by this loss that he was afraid to get excited over their new child. She stated that the husband didn't want God to take this baby "like He took the last one." My heart was broken by their misconception of God and their ignorance of His covenant of healing. We proceeded to tell them that it was not God who took their first baby. We also shared with them God's promise to bless our body found in Exodus 23:25-26. They did not even know that these Scriptures were in the Bible. Once we shared with them these truths, it shed a whole new light on God for them. Several months later, they had a beautiful healthy baby. The Bible promises that God will take away sickness from us. Stop holding on to what God wants to take away from you. Don't fight for the right to be sick. Embrace the covenant promise of healing today!

HEALING PRAYER

Father, I thank You for being Jehovah Rapha, the Great Physician. Just as You brought the Israelites out of Egyptian bondage, You brought me out of the bondage to the world's system. Through the blood of Jesus, I have been delivered from the curse of poverty, sickness, and death. Today I appropriate Your healing promises to every area of my life. I command mental, spiritual, emotional, and physical disorders to cease operation. I command all cancers and growths to die, and to dry up by the roots. Every condition of the blood and circulatory system is healed by the blood of Jesus. Thank You that I walk in perfect soundness in my body and soul. Now Father, I will avail myself as a vessel of honor to be used by You to liberate others from the bondage of sickness and disease. In the name of Jesus I pray. Amen!

Day 81

REBUKE THE DEVOURER

*And I will rebuke the devourer for your sakes, and
he shall not destroy the fruits of your ground; neither
shall your vine cast her fruit before the time in the
field, saith the Lord of hosts.* —Malachi 3:11

The enemy of our souls is a devourer. In the Scriptures he is likened to a roaring lion. The entire agenda of the devil is to kill, steal, and destroy. When we were in the world system, everything we had was subjected to the devourer—our money, our relationships, our mind, and our health. Like a cankerworm that eats away at a harvest, so the enemy loves to spoil our resources and our peace.

Unfortunately for the devil, however, we have a covenant with God. The Lord promises us in His Word that if we will obey Him, He will rebuke the devourer. In other words, He will prevent the enemy from destroying the fruits of our ground. What are the fruits of our ground? This is the Hebrew word *pĕriy*, and it means to produce, offspring, and actions (Strong's, H6529). This includes our children, our health, our money, our resources, and our ministry. God says that He will protect us and all we have. This is the best insurance that exists in the universe. Some people debate over whether Christians ought to rebuke the devil, but I believe that if God has rebuked the enemy, then we ought to agree with God and rebuke him too. Do not tolerate that wicked devourer in any area of your life. Healing is your covenant right. So why are you allowing the devil to eat away at your health? Your body is insured by God. It is time for you to make a claim against the enemy. The blood of Jesus testifies of your healing. Now that you know your rights, what are you going to do about it? The choice is yours.

HEALING PRAYER

Father, I thank You that healing is the children's bread. Through the blood of Jesus I have received salvation, which includes the right to walk in divine health. Today I declare that the devourer has been rebuked. I ask that You forgive me for anything I have done to open the door to the enemy, either through my ignorance or my disobedience. I make a claim against the enemy that he has infringed on my mind, body, and soul. I command all cankerworms assigned to me by the evil one to die. I command all cancers to dry up by their very roots right now in the name of Jesus. I refuse to allow the devil to steal from me again. Based on the authority of the Word of God, I declare that the enemy must return all resources, promises, and health he as obtained through illegal means, in the name of Jesus. Amen!

Day 82

STAND YOUR GROUND

Watch ye, stand fast in the faith, quit you like men, be strong. —1 Corinthians 16:13

Have you ever been in a fight or physical altercation? Unfortunately, I have been in several. As a child, I was very small and often picked on. I remember one particular conflict, where I had to face someone much bigger than myself. I was tempted to run, but I knew that if I ran I would be subjected to bullying for the remainder of the school year. Instead of running in fear, I decided to stand my ground. Those altercations in the schoolyard as a boy often remind me of spiritual warfare. The enemy is a bully who thrives off of fear, intimidation, and control. He believes that if he gives us enough resistance, we will give up. This strategy is carried out with such things as sickness and disease. These afflictions are designed to manipulate you into doubt and unbelief. Remember that faith is the shield of the spiritual realm; the moment you drop your shield in fear, you open yourself up to the fiery darts of the evil one. Paul the apostle, when writing to the Corinthian church, encouraged them to watch, stand fast in the faith, be brave, and be strong. The word *stand fast* comes from the Greek word *steko*, and it means to stand firm or stand your ground (Strong's, G4739). This is military terminology that refers to a soldier in the heat of the battle. The general would often tell his soldiers to "quit like men" or be brave and fight. Don't back down in fear, but put your shield up, your chest out, and move forward. One thing the devil doesn't count on is that you and I will resist him. He is so arrogant and prideful that he never plans for a counterattack. It is time for you to stand your ground. Do not allow sickness to manipulate you or intimidate you; it is simply a tool of the enemy. Remember, you have a bigger gun than he does.

HEALING PRAYER

Father, in the name of Jesus Christ, I declare that the weapons of my warfare are not carnal but mighty through God to the pulling down of strongholds. Today I cast down imaginations and every high thing that exalts itself against my knowledge of Jesus Christ. I take authority over the powers of darkness in the form of sickness and disease. I choose today to stand my ground in faith against the wiles of the enemy. I will not give into fear, discouragement, doubt, unbelief, or anxiety. I rejoice in Your Word, because Your Word has omnipotent power. This power works effectually in me to the fulfillment of Your promises in my life. Thank You, Father, for healing me in every fiber of my being. I am healed, whole, and delivered by the power of God and in the name of Jesus. Amen!

Day 83

KNOW YOUR RIGHTS

Now therefore ye are no more strangers and foreigners, but fellowcitizens with the saints, and of the household of God. —Ephesians 2:19

Citizenship is something most people are familiar with. There are only two ways to become a citizen of a nation: you must be born as a natural citizen or you must be made a citizen by the government. Before we came to Christ, the Bible says we were strangers and foreigners. What does it mean to be a stranger and a foreigner? If you have ever traveled outside of your homeland, you know that foreigners do not have the same rights and privileges as citizens. A foreigner usually speaks a different language or dialect and is not acclimated to the culture. We were alienated from the kingdom of God, we were foreigners, but now that we are born again, we have been made citizens. The word *fellowcitizen* in the Greek is the word *sympolitēs*, and it means to possess the same citizenship as others (Strong's, G4847). We have been adopted into the royal family of God, and as such we are entitled to certain rights and privileges under the New Covenant. The question is: Do you know your rights? There is nothing worse than being ignorant of your rights. Where there is ignorance there will always be abuse. The moment you discover your rights, you can put an end to all infringement and abuse. We are joint-heirs with Jesus. Do you know what that implies? We have access and co-ownership to everything Jesus possesses. The irony is that Jesus possesses all things. You have the right to be well. You have the right to be healed, and you have the right to be blessed. Know your rights! Enforce your rights.

HEALING PRAYER

Father, I thank You that through the blood of Jesus I have been given the right and privilege of citizenship. From this day forward I refuse to see myself or allow myself to be treated as an alien. Today I have been made aware of my rights through Your Word. Today I put an end to the infringement and abuse of the enemy in the form of sickness and disease. Thank You for the benefit of sonship. Lord, I realize my citizenship is in heaven and I am currently a part of the royal family of the kingdom of God, with God as Father, Jesus Christ as King and Elder Brother, the Holy Spirit as Governor and Comforter, and myself as brother, son, friend, and servant. Thank You for continual victory over the enemy, in the name of Jesus Christ. Amen!

Day 84

IT'S IN YOU!

But the anointing which ye have received of
Him abideth in you, and ye need not that
any man teach you: but as the same anointing
teacheth you of all things, and is truth, and
is no lie, and even as it hath taught you,
ye shall abide in Him. —1 John 2:27

Many years ago, when I first became a believer in Jesus, I was introduced to the term "the anointing." I heard it on Christian television and on Christian radio, and I read about it in Christian books. What was this anointing? I didn't have a clue what it was, but I desperately wanted it. Then in the summer of 1997, I received the baptism of the Holy Spirit. My life changed dramatically. Later I discovered that the anointing I was looking for was already inside of me. I have even better news than that—it's in you as well! The Scripture that transformed my life was 1 John 2:27, for in it I discovered that the anointing is resident in every believer. In fact, the Bible says we can't be taught it. This anointing is nothing other than the very presence of the Spirit of Truth, which is active and operative inside us. This is the same yoke-destroying anointing that rested upon the Messiah. This is the same anointing that empowered and enabled Jesus to go about doing good, and healing all those who were oppressed of the devil (see Acts 10:38). Did you realize that the same anointing of Jesus lives inside of you? You don't need anyone to lay hands on you or pray for you; you already have all the ingredients you need to experience divine healing. This same anointing was the very source of our Lord's power during His earthly ministry. This truth is a game changer. The Bible declares that greater is He that lives in you than he that lives in the world. Can I tell you a secret? You are far more powerful than the devil. You are more powerful than cancer or any other force that may array itself against the truth of God's Word. Now that you realize this anointing is already inside of you, you need to release it by faith. Lay hands on yourself, then go and lay hands on your loved ones. Heal the sick, cast out devils, cleanse the lepers, and raise the dead. Freely you have received, freely give.

HEALING PRAYER

Father, in the name of Jesus, I thank You for who You are and all You have done. I realize today that Your anointing abides in me, and it is truth. From this day forward I embrace the fact that I don't need any man to teach me how to operate in Your power, because the same Spirit that raised Jesus from the dead dwells in my spirit and He shall quicken my mortal flesh. Thank You that the yoke-destroying, burden-removing anointing is operating in me now, breaking and destroying the power of sickness once and for all. I no longer accept spiritual and physical sickness as a way of life. Today I activate the anointing inside of me to release power of divine healing and miracles right now, in the name of Jesus. Amen!

POWER IN HEAVEN AND EARTH

HEALING MEDITATION

And Jesus came and spake unto them, saying, All power is given unto me in heaven and in earth. Go ye therefore, and teach all nations, baptizing them in the name of the Father, and of the Son, and of the Holy Ghost. —Matthew 28:18-19

The simple truth is that God has given healing to the church as a gift of His great love and compassion. Not only do we have the covenant of healing through the blood of Jesus Christ, but we have been given the power to heal. I have often heard it said that some people have the gift of healing while others do not. This is not quite true. The Holy Spirit manifests the gift of healing as He wills, which is completely up to the Holy Spirit. For this reason, certain people may operate in healing in a greater measure and a more dynamic way than others, but this is a completely separate issue from the power and responsibility to heal that is given to every believer. Every single believer in Jesus Christ has been given the power to heal, whether the gift of healing is in manifestation or not. We no longer have an excuse to back down from our kingdom mandate to heal the sick (including ourselves). Some people may say, "Well, I don't have the gift of healing." This is completely unacceptable. You don't need the gift of healing to pray for the sick to be healed. What you need, however, is the faith to believe that all power in heaven and earth was given to the risen Christ, which is the same Christ who resides within you. In other words, God the Father has given Jesus all power, and He has commissioned us to go in His authority and power. Therefore, healing is not a matter of gifting or charisma; it is a matter of identity. We are one with Christ and He is one with us. He has all power in heaven and on earth, which means we can operate in the same power He did. Jesus cursed the fig tree; you can curse cancer. Jesus spoke to the wind and the waves and they obeyed His voice; you can speak to diabetes, blood disorders, and lupus and they too must obey your voice. It is time to demonstrate the power in heaven and earth.

HEALING PRAYER

Father, in the name of Jesus, I thank You that all power in heaven and earth was given unto Jesus, and because Jesus lives in me, I have all authority in heaven and on earth. Thank You for a supernatural paradigm shift, which enables me to see myself the way You see me. I declare that I am a person of supernatural power, enabling me to address all of the powers of darkness, especially sickness and disease. Thank You, Lord, that the law of the Spirit of life in Christ has made me free from the law of sin and death. I am sickness repellant. Wherever I go, healing manifests; whomever I pray for receives healing in the name of Jesus. Thank You for this spiritual reality working within me. Amen!

Day 86

BINDING AND LOOSING

HEALING MEDITATION

*And I will give unto thee the keys of the
kingdom of heaven: and whatsoever thou
shalt bind on earth shall be bound in heaven:
and whatsoever thou shalt loose on earth shall
be loosed in heaven.* —Matthew 16:19

One of the most profound revelations in my life was
an understanding of the authority of the believer.
Most of my life I was presented with a defeated and vic-
tim-oriented Christianity. Everything bad was attributed
to God and everything evil was attributed to the devil. I
was confused as to which side God was on. Religion and

tradition would have you believe God and the devil where dance partners. None of this was biblical. However, what is biblical is the truth that we as believers have been given awesome power and authority, not to accomplish our own purposes, but to advance the kingdom of God in the earth. The first time I learned about healing I was blown away at the idea that we could experience and perform the same miracles Jesus did while He was on earth. Can you imagine that? You should be able to because it is absolutely true. In fact, Jesus referred to something called the "keys of the kingdom." What were these? The word *keys* comes from the Greek word *kleis*, and it means "the power to open and shut," signifying various kinds of authority (Strong's, G2807). It is like a groundskeeper of a mansion; he has the authority to open every door in the mansion because he has the key ring. Jesus has given us the spiritual "key ring" to access realms and dimensions of the kingdom of God as they are necessary. This "key ring" is the revelation of Jesus Christ. When we have a revelation of Jesus (the King), it releases keys that enable us to take authority through binding and loosing. In other words, we can bind sickness and disease because we have revelation of the finished work of the cross, and we can release healing and wholeness because we know Him as the Great Physician. Whatever we bind is bound.

HEALING PRAYER

Father, I thank You for giving me the keys of the kingdom of God, so that whatever I bind on earth will have been bound in heaven, and whatever I loose on earth will have been loosed in heaven. We are not victims of the doctor's report or our environment, but we have been supernaturally empowered to affect change in both the earthly and heavenly realms. I bind sickness, including lupus, diabetes, fibromyalgia, HIV/AIDS, heart disease, cancer, MS, Crohn's, kidney failure, liver failure, hypertension, and Parkinson's disease. Right now, I loose healing, health, wholeness, restoration, hope, peace, soundness of mind, and new body parts in the name of Jesus. Amen!

SEATED WITH CHRIST

HEALING MEDITATION

*And hath raised us up together, and
made us sit together in heavenly places
in Christ Jesus.* —Ephesians 2:6

One of the most profound books in the Bible is the book of Ephesians. It is quite theologically empowering and spiritually rewarding. I am strengthened and encouraged every time I read it. In it we see the positional reality of us as believers. In the second chapter, Paul asserts that we have been made to sit together with Him (Jesus) in heavenly places. What does this mean? Many times in the Western world, we may have a difficult time wrapping our mind around certain concepts. To a person in ancient Rome or Palestine, however, this would mean a significant deal. Kings and dignitaries expressed their benevolence by sitting at the same table or court with their friends and constituents. It was a sign of deep intimacy and respect. Interestingly enough, it was also as sign of equality. To sit with a king meant that you were a part of his family. King Jesus has caused us to sit together with Him, which symbolizes fellowship and equal authority. Most conservative theologians would cringe at the thought of being on the same level as Jesus, but this is what the Bible explicitly states. We are no longer wretched sinners. We are joint-heirs with Jesus. Why is this so important? When you are praying for your healing or ministering healing to others, you need to be aware of the way God sees you. If you approach God as a terrible sinner who doesn't deserve anything, there is no way you are going to confidently appropriate the promises of God. On the other hand, if you realize you are a son or daughter who has been made righteous by the blood of the Lamb, and who is seated next to Christ in the heavenly realm, then you will have the confidence you need to receive from Him.

HEALING PRAYER

Father, in the name of Jesus, I thank You that You are the Creator of the Universe, and You have chosen to have a relationship with me through Your Son Jesus. Today I accept my spiritual position as seated with You in heavenly places in Christ. I am not just seated with Christ, but I am seated in Christ, which means I carry the full authority and power of Jesus Christ everywhere I go. Thank You, Lord, for Your goodness toward me. Thank You, Jesus, for inviting me to Your banquet table for all eternity. From this day forward I choose to see myself in a whole new life. I am no longer a victim, I no longer make excuses for challenges in my life, and I no longer accept sickness as a normal way of life. In the name of Jesus I pray, amen.

Day 88

REDEEMED FROM THE CURSE

HEALING MEDITATION

Christ hath redeemed us from the curse of the law,
being made a curse for us: for it is written, Cursed
is every one that hangeth on a tree: that the blessing
of Abraham might come on the Gentiles through
Jesus Christ; that we might receive the promise of
the Spirit through faith. —Galatians 3:13-14

Deuteronomy 21:22-23 says: "And if a man have committed a sin worthy of death, and he be to be put to death, and thou hang him on a tree: his body shall not remain all night upon the tree, but thou shalt in any wise bury him that day; (for he that is hanged is accursed of God;) that thy land be not defiled, which the Lord thy God giveth thee for an inheritance." Death by the tree was one of the worst penalties in the Old and New Testaments. In Rome, during the time of Christ, crucifixion was deemed capital punishment. It was reserved only for the worst of criminals. Those who received this punishment were considered cursed by God. Two thousand years ago Jesus became a curse for us. He did nothing to deserve the punishment He received. We were the ones who deserved to die on that cross, but Christ became our substitutionary sacrifice. He paid the ultimate price for our healing and our freedom. Through this violent act of grace, those of us who accepted this sacrifice by faith were thrust into the kingdom of God. This is why you no longer have the right to be sick, because the price for your healing was so enormous that no one could pay it except Christ. How dare you remain in your sickness. I would go as far as to say that to passively accept sickness in your body is to defy the work of the cross and ultimately sin against God. I don't know about you, but I don't want to sin against God. We have been redeemed from the curse of sin, sickness, and death; it's time to start acting like it.

HEALING PRAYER

Father, I thank You for sending Your Son Jesus Christ to die in my place, to bear the penalty of my sin, and to take my place on the cross. I thank You now that I am no longer under the curse of the law, but through the body of Jesus I am blessed. Lord, I thank You that the penalty of sin—poverty, sickness, bareness, and death—has been abolished through Jesus. I receive the sacrifice of Jesus by faith and, therefore, I have been grafted into the kingdom of God. By faith, I receive the blessing of Abraham; therefore, I am righteous, favored, and blessed. I thank You, Lord, that the Spirit of life that raised Jesus from the dead dwells in me. I thank You that the supernatural life of God reigns in me through the name of Jesus. Amen.

LOOK UNTO JESUS

HEALING MEDITATION

*Looking unto Jesus the author and finisher
of our faith; who for the joy that was set
before Him endured the cross, despising the
shame, and is set down at the right hand
of the throne of God.* —Hebrews 12:2

In Matthew 14 the Bible gives the famous account of Jesus walking on water, "And Peter answered Him and said, Lord, if it be Thou, bid me come unto Thee on the water" (Matthew 14:28). Peter loved Jesus to the best of his ability, and when he saw Jesus walking on water, he wanted to be with Him where He was. Peter had faith, but his faith was not mature yet; it was undeveloped. Immature faith only operates when it has no other choice. The circumstances in the boat forced him outside of his comfort zone. Some of us are like that—we believe God when the conditions are right and when we are in the right environment. As Jesus bid Peter to come, a miraculous thing took place— Peter walked on the water just like Jesus. This is amazing to me. Notice that as long as he set his eyes on Jesus, he could do the same thing Jesus was doing. He could walk in the power of God. But the moment he took his eyes off of Jesus, he began to sink. The Bible tells us that we are to look to Jesus. The word *look* means to turn the eyes away from other things and fix them on something else. God is telling you to turn your eyes away from your circumstances, your limitations, and your fears, and to set your eyes on Jesus. Remember, you become filled with whatever you set your eyes on. When we refuse to look at sickness, and instead gaze on the Living Word, we become filled with His supernatural power. Jesus is the author and finisher of our faith. Whatever God has begun in you, He is faithful to complete it. God never begins a project He does not intend to see through till the end. Look unto Jesus and nothing else.

HEALING PRAYER

Dear Lord Jesus, I fix my eyes upon You and I refuse to look at anything or anyone else. I will not look at my physical limitations, my past, my sin, or any other thing that would seek to distract me from looking upon Your face, being overwhelmed by Your beauty. Lord, You are truly beautiful to me, and I desire more than anything to see You as You are. Thank You for being my Healer and my Deliverer. I know I have nothing to fear because what You started You will surely finish. Thank You for Your miraculous power working in and through me right now. I declare I have Your faith, and Your faith will never fail. Thank You, Lord. In Jesus's name I pray, amen!

RECEIVE YOUR HEALING

HEALING MEDITATION

And all things, whatsoever ye shall ask in prayer, believing, ye shall receive. —Matthew 21:22

Several years ago I was in a place where I thought sickness was normal. I saw so much of it that I came to accept it. I knew more Christians who were sick than people in the world. When I reflect back on where I was in my mind, I realize what a disturbing place it was. While I was in that place, I realized that what I was seeing was not the will of God for my life. As a matter of fact, I remember when I met my wife, she struggled with migraine headaches. One day we were together and she complained of pain in her head. I went to her almost unconsciously and said, "Peace, be still. You are healed in Jesus's name." Instantly the headache went away. She has never had that struggle since. Little did I know that God was seeding our ministry of healing and deliverance. The word *receive* comes from the Greek word *lambano* and it means to take a thing due or to possess (Strong's, G2983). Like most of you reading this book, I realized there had to be more to being a Christian than singing songs and going to church. There was a life of healing and wholeness that was made available through the cross. God wants us whole; we have to possess the wholeness God made available to us in Christ. The first thing we have to do is become convinced that healing is the children's bread. The second thing we must do is come to the revelation that it has already been accomplished for us on the cross. Lastly, we must take the initiative and appropriate the Word of God in our bodies. This requires us taking an aggressive stand against sickness and for the promises of God. Receive your healing right now in the name of Jesus!

HEALING PRAYER

Father, in the name of Jesus Christ, I thank You that because of Christ's blood You hear me. Thank You, Father, that I am healed completely through the atoning work of Jesus Christ on the cross. Every area of my body must submit to the lordship of Jesus. Every cell in my body functions perfectly. Every atom in my body is under Your control and authority. I am healed and whole in the name of Jesus. First Peter 2:24 declares that I have been healed by His stripes. I am healed in Jesus's name. I walk in the divine health You have ordained for my life. Thank You, Jesus Christ, for being my Healer. I release any and all offenses in my heart that would hinder my faith from operating the way that it should. Thank You, Lord, for Your grace! In Jesus's name I pray all of these things, amen.

ABOUT THE AUTHOR

At the tender age of 15, Pastor Kynan committed his life to Jesus Christ and was subsequently filled with the Holy Spirit. After getting involved in his local church, God made His call manifest to Kynan audibly. For many years, he served in the local church and was involved with various ministries. But after running from the call of God, he was finally arrested by the Holy Spirit. Several years ago the Lord told Kynan to begin a teaching ministry in Tampa, Florida, where the vision for Grace and Peace Global Fellowship was birthed.

Paul wrote, "For if by one man's offense death reined by one; much more they which receive abundance of grace and of the gift of righteousness shall reign in life by one, Jesus Christ" (Romans 5:17). This is the vision and mission of our ministry: to see the person, power, and presence of Jesus Christ manifested in the lives of people everywhere so they will reign in life. Through this ministry we desire to see millions of souls saved and restored through the gospel of Jesus Christ. We accomplish this mission by proclaiming the unadulterated, life-changing Word of God. Our outreach ministry serves as the catalyst to spread this message. Every week we provide resources to people so they might become more conscious of Christ's love for them and enter into the fullness of His finished work, thereby being positioned to walk in their God-ordained assignment, namely the great commission, as outlined in Matthew 28:19-20.

Our weekly podcast (FaithTalk) serves as a platform to discuss various issues in the body of Christ and around the world, shedding light on those issues through the illumination of God's Word. We are committed to spreading the gospel through our preaching ministry, speaking engagements, teaching resources, and Internet and media platforms.

To date we have reached countless numbers of people with the gospel. Through the combined efforts of our weekly outreach ministry and new media resources, we have exposed thousands to the gospel of grace every single week. Currently we are communicating God's Word to people in North America, India, Haiti, and Nigeria. We are engaging in several outreach efforts, which have a global impact as well.

Pastor Kynan is committed to allowing the power and anointing of the Holy Spirit to flow through him and touch God's people. He is a committed husband, mentor, and father to two beautiful daughters: Ella and Naomi. For information on booking, prayer requests, or supporting this ministry, write to:

Kynan Bridges Ministries
P.O. Box 159
Ruskin, FL 33575
1.800.516.7038
Or visit us at:
www.kynanbridges.org